World Book's Documenting History
Women's Right to Vote

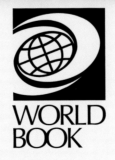

WORLD BOOK

a Scott Fetzer company
Chicago

www.worldbookonline.com

World Book, Inc.
233 N. Michigan Avenue
Chicago, IL 60601
U.S.A.

For information about other World Book publications, visit our Website at **http://www.worldbookonline.com**
or call **1-800-WORLDBK (967-5325).**

For information about sales to schools and libraries, call **1-800-975-3250 (United States)**, or **1-800-837-5365 (Canada).**

Library of Congress Cataloging-in-Publication Data

Women's right to vote.
        p. cm. -- (World Book's documenting history)
    Includes bibliographical references and index.
    Summary: "A history of the women's suffrage movement throughout the world, based on primary source documents and other historical artifacts. Features include period art works and photographs; excerpts from literary works, letters, speeches, broadcasts, and diaries; summary boxes; a timeline; maps; and a list of additional resources"-- Provided by publisher.
    ISBN 978-0-7166-1508-8
    1. Women--Suffrage--History--Juvenile literature. 2. Women's rights--History--Juvenile literature. I. World Book, Inc.
JF851.W66 2011
324.6'23--dc22
                                    2010026711

World Book's Documenting History
Set ISBN 978-0-7166-1498-2
Printed in Malaysia by TWP Sdn Bhd, JohorBahru
1st printing September 2010

Contents

Early Years in America

SUFFRAGE IS THE RIGHT TO VOTE AS A CITIZEN IN PUBLIC ELECTIONS. In general, gaining suffrage has taken longer and been harder for women than for men. Until about 200 years ago, only small groups of people could vote. Traditionally in Europe and its colonies, only men who owned a certain amount of property had suffrage. Lawmakers believed that property owners had enough stake in society to vote responsibly and enough independence to vote without being influenced by powerful landlords or employers. In the late 1700's and the 1800's, these assumptions began to change. Governments started removing property requirements and religious and ethnic restrictions on suffrage. However, most lawmakers still viewed women as dependent on husbands or male relatives and incapable of handling the responsibility of voting.

In 1789, when the United States Constitution went into effect, about 60 percent of white men in the new nation could vote. Many white men and most African Americans, Native Americans, and women were excluded. One state, New Jersey, allowed women who met its property requirements to vote. But in 1807, New Jersey passed a law limiting suffrage to white men.

I long to hear that you have declared an independency—and, by the way, in the new Code of Laws, which I suppose it will be necessary for you to make, I desire you would Remember the Ladies, and be more generous and favourable to them than your ancestors. Do not put such unlimited power into the hands of the Husbands. Remember, all Men would be tyrants if they could. If particular care and attention is not paid to the Ladies we are determined to foment [foster] a Rebellion, and will not hold ourselves bound by any Laws in which we have no voice, or Representation.
Abigail Adams to John Adams, March 31, 1776

As to your extraordinary Code of Laws, I cannot but laugh. . . . Depend upon it. We know better than to repeal [do away with] our masculine systems.
John Adams to Abigail Adams, April 14, 1776

I can not say that I think you are very generous to the Ladies; for whilst you are proclaiming peace and good will to Men, Emancipating [freeing] all Nations, you insist upon retaining absolute power over wives.
Abigail Adams to John Adams,
May 7, 1776

◀ A series of letters written between American lawyer and founding father John Adams (1735-1826) and his wife Abigail Adams (1744-1818) in 1776 contains a spirited discussion about what should be included in the laws of the new, independent nation they both wanted. Abigail thought women should have equal educational opportunities and greater protection under the law. She compared women's desire for such rights to the colonists' desire to establish their liberty and defend their political rights. John greatly respected Abigail's opinions, including her views on politics, but like other men of his time, he considered the idea of women in government to be laughable.

John Adams was a prominent supporter of American independence from Great Britain (later the United Kingdom). Adams signed the Declaration of Independence in 1776. He later served as a diplomat and as vice president of the United States before he was elected the nation's second president in 1796.

▶ American painter Gilbert Stuart (1755-1828) created this portrait of Abigail Adams about 1800-1815. Adams had little formal education. However, she developed her literary skills and became her husband's ally and adviser. Frequently separated from John, she maintained a lively correspondence with him and urged him to incorporate women's rights into the laws of the new republic.

NOW YOU KNOW

- In the U.S. in the late 1700's, voting was a right held mostly by white men who owned property.
- Women were not considered equal as citizens and were not permitted to vote.
- Abigail Adams supported equal education and greater legal protection for women.

The French Revolution

REVOLUTION BROKE OUT IN FRANCE IN 1789. For years, there had been growing discontent there with the absolute rule of the king and with the nobility. A number of French reformers joined together in 1789 and formed a legislative body called the National Assembly of France. Partly inspired by the American Revolution (1775-1783), the Assembly adopted the Declaration of the Rights of Man, which declared that citizens should have political rights, including suffrage. The Declaration did not specifically include women. When France's new constitution went into effect in 1791, it distinguished between "active" and "passive" citizens. Only men could be active citizens with the right to vote and hold public office. Women, servants, and others viewed as "dependent" on other people were considered passive citizens and had no voting rights.

1

The common good, above all that of women, demands that they do not *aspire* [hope] to the *exercise* [use] of potential rights and functions. . . . Is it not apparent that their delicate *constitutions* [natures], their gentle dispositions, the numerous duties of maternity, must always distance them from powerful commitments and strenuous duties, and call them to peaceful occupations and household cares?

Charles Maurice de
Talleyrand-Perigord,
Prince de Benevent, 1791

◀ In a report to the National Constituent Assembly in 1791, the French statesman Talleyrand (1754-1838) argues that women are too delicate to participate in government. The National Constituent Assembly was successor to the National Assembly.

2

The Rights of Women

Article 1
Woman is born free and lives equal to man in her rights. Social distinctions can only be based on the common utility. . .

Article VI
The law must be the expression of the general will; all female and male citizens must contribute either personally or through their representatives to its formation; it must be the same for all: male and female citizens, being equal in the eyes of the law, must be equally admitted to all honors, petitions [requests], and public employment according to their capacity and without other distinctions besides those of their virtues and talents.

Olympe de Gouges,
Declaration of the Rights
of Woman, 1791

▶ French playwright and revolutionary Olympe de Gouges (1748?-1793) wrote the Declaration of the Rights of Woman in 1791 to protest the exclusion of women from the Declaration of the Rights of Man. Gouges's manifesto imitated the format of the Declaration of the Rights of Man, but she rewrote each *article* (section) to apply to women. Her political views gained her enemies, and she was executed on Nov. 3, 1793, by *guillotine* (a machine for chopping off heads).

à Versailles à Versailles du 5 Octobre 1789.

▲ An engraving titled "To Versailles, To Versailles" from the late 1700's illustrates women marching on Versailles on Oct. 5-6, 1789. A large group of women, angered by the scarcity and high price of food, marched 12 miles (19 kilometers) in wind and rain from Paris to the royal palace at Versailles. They forced the king and queen and the National Assembly to return to Paris the following day and to promise to lower the price of food.

NOW YOU KNOW

- During the French Revolution (1789-1799), the National Assembly adopted the Declaration of the Rights of Man to ensure political rights for French citizens.
- The French Constitution, however, did not count women as active citizens in a political sense.
- The women of Paris played an important role in launching the French Revolution.

Reactions to the Revolution

THE FRENCH REVOLUTION GENERATED GREAT INTEREST AND CONCERN throughout Europe. Debate was especially fierce in Britain, where freedom of expression was more established than in many other countries. In 1790, the British statesman Edmund Burke (1729-1797) wrote an influential book denouncing the French Revolution and its effects on society. In response, the British writer and agitator Thomas Paine (1737-1809) published his famous *The Rights of Man* (1791-1792), demanding representative government for France. Even more revolutionary was the pioneering British author Mary Wollstonecraft (1759-1797). Her book *A Vindication of the Rights of Woman* (1792) challenged male revolutionaries to see that a real revolution must include equal rights for women.

◀ A portrait of Thomas Paine painted by American artist John Wesley Jarvis (1781-1840) about 1806. Paine was a British pamphleteer, agitator, and writer on politics and religion. He supported the American and French revolutions and progressive movements in Britain. When Paine published his *Rights of Man* in 1791 and 1792, the British government considered it too radical and suppressed the work. Paine was tried for treason and outlawed in December 1792, but he had already gone to France and become a French citizen.

▶ A passage from Mary Wollstonecraft's book *A Vindication of the Rights of Woman* questions those who deny women the same civil and political rights as men when women possess the same capacity for reason as men. Wollstonecraft dedicated her book to the French statesman and reformer Talleyrand.

Who made man the exclusive judge, if woman partake with him the gift of reason? . . . [tyrants] are all eager to crush reason; yet always assert that they *usurp* [seize] its throne only to be useful. Do you not act as similar part, when you *force* all women, by denying them civil and political rights, to remain *immured* [shut up] in their families, groping in the dark?

Mary Wollstonecraft, 1792

◀ A black-and-white print of Mary Wollstonecraft based on a portrait by John Opie (1761-1807) from around 1791. Wollstonecraft was a revolutionary writer and philosopher. She urged a "revolution in female manners," arguing that society confined women's bodies and minds and that a more moral and just society would give women the same rights as men had. Wollstonecraft challenged the men who drafted a new French constitution in 1791 to ensure that boys and girls receive the same education. This would enable women to play an equal role in society and to understand and use their political rights.

▶ A poem by the Scottish poet Robert Burns (1759-1796) suggests that society would benefit by focusing less on war and more on women's rights. But the poem later names these rights as protection by men, the *decorum* (proper behavior) of men, and the admiration of men, not political rights. Burns's poem mentions works by Thomas Paine and Mary Wollstonecraft. The final line of the poem also makes reference to a French revolutionary song.

While Europe's eye is fix'd on mighty things,
The fate of Empires and the fall of Kings;
While quacks [frauds] of State must each produce his plan,
And even children lisp [speak] the Rights of Man;
Amid this mighty fuss just let me mention,
The Rights of Woman merit some attention.

from "The Rights of Woman" (1792)

NOW YOU KNOW

- The French Revolution sparked debate throughout Europe.
- Thomas Paine published *The Rights of Man* in support of the French Revolution.
- Mary Wollstonecraft supported political rights for women as well as men in her book *A Vindication of the Rights of Woman*.

The Chartists

IN THE EARLY 1800'S, THE UNITED KINGDOM WAS ONE OF A FEW COUNTRIES with a parliamentary government. Yet only a small number of people could vote. In 1832, following public protests, the British Parliament extended voting rights to include middle-class men and gave more representation to the nation's growing cities. A new movement called Chartism demanded suffrage for all men and other reforms. Some Chartists supported political rights for women, and some women formed their own Chartist societies. The Chartists collected millions of signatures on petitions and held huge meetings and marches. Soldiers brutally broke up Chartist gatherings and Chartist leaders were jailed, exiled, or executed.

▶ "Address of the Female Political Union of Newcastle-upon-Tyne to Their Fellow Countrywomen" was published in the Chartist newspaper the *Northern Star* on Feb. 9, 1839. The author urges women to get involved in politics and support broader suffrage to improve the lives of their families.

▼ A cartoon published in the British humor magazine *Punch* in 1848 recommends "how to treat the female Chartists"—by scaring them away with such pests as rats, mice, and cockroaches. Some of the most enthusiastic supporters of the Chartists were women, who attended meetings in great numbers. Opponents of the Chartists often depicted women supporters as ugly, unfeminine, or easily frightened.

1

We have been told that the *province* [proper work] of woman is her home, and that the field of politics should be left to men; this we deny. . . . Is it not true that the interests of our fathers, husbands, and brothers, ought to be ours? . . . there is no remedy but the just measure of allowing every citizen of the United Kingdom, the right of voting in the election of the members of Parliaments, who have to make the laws that he has to be governed by, and grant the taxes that he has to pay . . . This is what the working men of England, Ireland, and Scotland, are struggling for, and we have banded ourselves together in union to assist them; and we call on all our fellow-countrywomen to join us.

Northern Star, 1839

2

HOW TO TREAT THE FEMALE CHARTISTS.

3

Ought women interfere in the political affairs of the country? . . . I do most distinctly and *unequivocally* [without doubt] say—YES! And for the following reasons:

First, Because she has a natural right.

Second, Because she has a civil right.

Third, Because she has a political right.

Fourth, Because it is a duty *imperative* [urgent] on her.

Fifth, Because it is *derogatory* [belittling] to the divine will to neglect so imperative a duty.

R. J. Richardson, 1840

◀ R. J. Richardson (1808-1861) wrote his pamphlet *The Rights of Women* in 1840, while in prison for social activism. Richardson was a Chartist leader from Manchester, England, who supported women's rights. He argued that the Bible and natural law supported the right of women, especially the poorest and most exploited women, to have a voice in government. Richardson sought the vote for single and widowed women. He believed that married women gained representation through their husbands' votes.

4

The Six Points
OF THE
PEOPLE'S
CHARTER.

1. A VOTE for every man twenty-one years of age, of sound mind, and not undergoing punishment for crime.

2. THE BALLOT.—To protect the elector in the exercise of his vote.

3. No PROPERTY QUALIFICATION for Members of Parliament —thus enabling the constituencies to return the man of their choice, be he rich or poor.

4. PAYMENT OF MEMBERS, thus enabling an honest trades-man, working man, or other person, to serve a constituency, when taken from his business to attend to the interests of the country.

5. EQUAL CONSTITUENCIES, securing the same amount of representation for the same number of electors, instead of allowing small constituencies to swamp the votes of large ones.

6. ANNUAL PARLIAMENTS, thus presenting the most effectual check to bribery and intimidation, since though a constituency might be bought once in seven years (even with the ballot), no purse could buy a constituency (under a system of universal suffrage) in each ensuing twelvemonth; and since members, when elected for a year only, would not be able to defy and betray their constituents as now.

▶ In *The People's Charter,* published in 1838, the Chartists made six demands: (1) suffrage for most men age 21 or older; (2) a secret ballot; (3) no property qualifications for members of Parliament; (4) payment of members of Parliament; (5) equal electoral districts; and (6) annual parliamentary elections. The Chartists did not achieve all of their goals. However, most of their demands were eventually met. Today, most British citizens who are at least 18 years old may vote, and there are regular, though not annual, parliamentary elections.

NOW YOU KNOW

- In the 1800's, most people in the United Kingdom could not vote.
- The Chartists wanted universal male suffrage, and a few supported political rights for women.
- Many women who believed that suffrage would improve people's lives supported the Chartists.

The Abolition Movement

MANY PROGRESSIVE-MINDED PEOPLE became involved in the *abolition* (antislavery) movement in the early 1800's. In 1807, the British Parliament outlawed the slave trade in the British Empire. The same year, the U.S. Congress prohibited the importation of slaves into the United States. The U.S. law took effect in 1808. However, buying and selling slaves remained legal in many U.S. states. In the 1830's, abolitionists focused their efforts on ending slavery throughout the country. Women who became involved in this struggle often were excluded from abolitionist meetings or forbidden to speak publicly.

1

But I ask no favors for my sex. I surrender not our claim to equality. All I ask of our brethren is that they will take their feet from off our necks, and permit us to stand upright on the ground which God has designed for us to occupy. . . .

Now to me it is perfectly clear, that whatsoever it is morally right for a man to do, it is morally right for a woman to do.

The Spectator, 1837

◀ In 1837, *The Spectator*, a Massachusetts newspaper, published a series of letters written by the American social reformer Sarah Grimké (1792-1873). The letters were published in the book *Letters on the Equality of the Sexes and the Condition of Women* in 1838. Grimké addressed the letters to Mary S. Parker, the president of the Boston Female Anti-Slavery Society. The letters also were published in *The Liberator*, a newspaper published by the American journalist and social reformer William Lloyd Garrison (1805-1879).

2

3

▲ The Grimké sisters, Sarah (above left) and Angelina (1805-1879), were from a slave-owning family in South Carolina, but they hated slavery. They became abolitionists and members of the Quakers (the Religious Society of Friends). Sarah clashed with Quaker elders because of their discrimination against black members. The Grimké sisters' experiences led them to speak out for women's equality.

4

As Mrs. Mott and I walked home . . . we resolved to hold a convention as soon as we returned home, and form a society to advocate the rights of women. These were the first women I had ever met who believed in the equality of the sexes . . . The acquaintance of Lucretia Mott, who was a broad, liberal thinker on politics, religion, and all questions of reform, opened to me a new world of thought. . . . It was intensely gratifying to hear all that, through years of doubt, I had dimly thought, so freely discussed by other women . . .

Elizabeth Cady Stanton, 1897

◀ Elizabeth Cady Stanton (1815-1902), an early leader of the women's rights movement in the United States, comments on her experiences at the first World Anti-Slavery Convention, in June 1840. Stanton attended the convention in London as the wife of one of the delegates. While there, she met American social reformer Lucretia Mott (1793-1880). Mott was one of several female delegates to the convention, but the men in charge of the meeting refused to seat any female delegates.

5

▶ Sojourner Truth (1797?-1883) was one of the best-known abolitionists of her day. She was the first black woman *orator* (public speaker) to speak out against slavery. Her original name was Isabella Baumfree. Baumfree was born a slave in New York. She became free in 1828 under a New York law that banned slavery. In 1843, Baumfree experienced what she regarded as a command from God to preach. She then took the name Soujourner Truth and began traveling and speaking about religion and the abolition of slavery.

NOW YOU KNOW

- Many antislavery campaigners thought it was wrong for women to speak and campaign against slavery.
- The Grimké sisters were leading abolitionists and supporters of women's rights.
- Sojourner Truth became the first black woman to speak out publicly against slavery.

The Declaration of Sentiments

THE DECLARATION OF SENTIMENTS, also known as the Seneca Falls Declaration, was a document drafted mainly by Lucretia Mott and Elizabeth Cady Stanton that outlined women's complaints and the rights that they demanded. The most controversial right was women's suffrage. The declaration was presented at the nation's first women's rights convention, held in Seneca Falls, New York, on July 19-20, 1848. During the meeting, organized by Mott and Stanton, more than 300 women and men debated issues of women's rights. The final declaration was signed by 68 women and 32 men.

1

We hold these truths to be self-evident: that all men and women are created equal; that they are *endowed* [granted] by their Creator with certain *inalienable* [undeniable] rights; that among these are life, liberty, and the pursuit of happiness; that to secure these rights governments are instituted, *deriving* [obtaining] their just powers from the consent of the governed . . . .

The history of mankind is a history of repeated injuries and *usurpations* [unjust seizures] on the part of man toward woman, having in direct object the establishment of an absolute tyranny over her. . . .

He has never permitted her to exercise her inalienable right to the *elective franchise* [the right to vote].

He has compelled her to submit to laws, in the formation of which she had no voice.

from the Declaration
of Sentiments, 1848

◀ The Declaration of Sentiments was modeled on the Declaration of Independence, which states, "We hold these truths to be self-evident, that all men are created equal . . ."

2

When our Fathers made out their famous bill of impeachment [accusation] against England, they specified eighteen grievances [complaints]. When the women of this country surveyed the situation at their first convention, they found they had precisely that number, and quite similar in character; and reading over the old revolutionary arguments of Jefferson, Patrick Henry, Otis and Adams, they found that they applied remarkably well to their case. The same arguments made in this country for extending suffrage from time to time, to white men, native-born citizens, without property and education, and to foreigners; the same used by John Bright in England, to extend to a million new voters, and the same used by the Republican Party to enfranchise [give the vote to] a million Black men in the South, all these arguments we have today to offer for women. . . .

Elizabeth Cady
Stanton, 1869

▶ In a speech delivered at the first National Woman Suffrage Convention, held in Washington, D.C., on Jan. 19-20, 1869, Elizabeth Cady Stanton presented arguments for adding an amendment to the U.S. Constitution giving women the right to vote.

3

Elizabeth Cady Stanton and her daughter, Harriet. from a daguerreotype 1856.

◄ Elizabeth Cady Stanton photographed with her daughter Harriet, one of her seven children, in 1856. Stanton devoted herself to the causes of abolition and women's rights for more than 50 years. In 1878, Stanton persuaded Senator Aaron A. Sargent of California to sponsor an amendment to the U.S. Constitution giving women the right to vote. However, the U.S. Congress did not approve the amendment until 1919, 17 years after Stanton's death. In 1920, it became the 19th Amendment to the Constitution.

NOW YOU KNOW

- Lucretia Mott and Elizabeth Cady Stanton organized the first women's rights convention at Seneca Falls, New York, in 1848.
- The Seneca Falls convention drafted the Declaration of Sentiments, modeled on the Declaration of Independence.
- The 19th Amendment to the U.S. Constitution granted suffrage to American women in 1920.

Susan B. Anthony

THE SENECA FALLS CONVENTION MARKED THE START of the women's suffrage movement in the United States. The women who attended the convention were not just concerned with voting but also with improving women's status in society. They pressed for a whole range of reforms, especially concerning marriage and property rights. Women's rights campaigners remained involved in the abolition movement and supported the Union side in the American Civil War (1861-1865). They welcomed constitutional amendments that ended slavery throughout the United States in 1865 and gave former slaves citizenship in 1868. In 1869, the U.S. Congress proposed a bill that would extend suffrage to black men, but not to women. In 1870, this bill became the 15th Amendment to the Constitution. In 1869, Elizabeth Cady Stanton and American social reformer Susan B. Anthony (1820-1906) formed the National Woman Suffrage Association to work for a women's suffrage amendment to the Constitution. Like Stanton, Anthony died more than a decade before American women received the right to vote.

◀ Susan Brownell Anthony came from a family of Massachusetts Quakers who believed in the equality of men and women. While working for the *temperance movement,* the campaign to curb the use of alcoholic beverages, Anthony became increasingly aware that women did not have the same rights as men. Anthony met Elizabeth Cady Stanton in 1851 and soon became devoted to the women's rights movement. A powerful speaker noted for her energy and organizational skills, Anthony was also a single woman and thus better able than Stanton to travel and organize for her cause. In addition to women's suffrage, Anthony supported reform in the areas of women's education, property rights, and dress. For a time, she wore pants called *bloomers,* which became a symbol of the women's rights movement.

2

May it please your honour, I shall never pay a dollar of your unjust penalty. All the stock in trade I possess is a $10,000 debt, incurred by publishing my paper—The Revolution . . . the sole object of which is to educate all women to do precisely as I have done, rebel against your man-made, unjust, unconstitutional forms of law, that tax, fine, imprison, and hang women, while they deny them the right of representation in the government . . .

Susan B. Anthony, 1873

◀ Susan B. Anthony addresses a court in 1873, after being found guilty of unlawful voting. Anthony, her three sisters, and several other women cast ballots in Rochester, New York, in the U.S. presidential election on Nov. 5, 1872. Anthony argued that according to the 14th Amendment to the Constitution, which prohibited states from denying certain rights to U.S. citizens, women could vote. Anthony was fined $100 plus the cost of her trial. She never paid the fine. However, no further legal action was taken against her, that she might have no grounds for appealing to a higher court.

▶ Susan B. Anthony presented the Declaration of Rights for Women by the National Woman Suffrage Association at a centennial celebration of U.S. independence in Philadelphia on July 4, 1876. The association had requested permission to present its declaration to the government during the celebration proceedings. The request was denied. But on the day of the celebration, Anthony and some fellow association members boldly approached Thomas W. Ferry, the U.S. senator from Michigan, during the ceremony, and publicly presented him with the declaration in Philadelphia's Independence Square. Anthony then proceeded to read the declaration aloud to a crowd in front of Independence Hall, where the Declaration of Independence had been adopted 100 years earlier.

3

Our faith is firm and *unwavering* [unhesitating] in the broad principles of human rights proclaimed in 1776, not only as . . . truths, but as the corner stones of a republic. Yet we cannot forget, even in this glad hour, that while all men of every race, and clime, and condition, have been invested with the full rights of citizenship under our hospitable flag all women still suffer the *degradation* [shame] of *disenfranchisement* [being unable to vote].

from the Declaration of Rights for Women by the National Woman Suffrage Association

NOW YOU KNOW

- In 1870, the 15th Amendment to the Constitution granted black men, but not women, suffrage.
- Susan B. Anthony and Elizabeth Cady Stanton formed the National Woman Suffrage Association in 1869.
- Susan B. Anthony and several other women were arrested for voting illegally in 1872.

Women and Parliament

IN THE 1800'S, MORE AND MORE BRITISH MEN GAINED THE VOTE as a series of reform bills nearly eliminated property qualifications for voting. During this period, the British philosopher and parliamentarian John Stuart Mill (1806-1873) and his wife, Harriet Taylor Mill (1807-1858), both wrote in support of women's suffrage. In May 1867, two years after he was elected to Parliament, Mill tried to amend (change) the new Representation of the People Bill to extend the vote to women who owned property. Only 73 of the 658 members of Parliament voted in favor of the amendment. During the next 40 years, British women gradually gained some voting rights in local elections, but they still could not vote for representatives to Parliament.

1

> No vote can be given by lunatics, idiots, *minors* [children], *aliens* [foreigners], females, persons convicted of *perjury* [lying while under oath in a trial] . . . bribery . . . or by those *attainted* [stained by] . . .felony, or outlawed in a criminal suit.
>
> Sir Charles Dilke, quoting
> Sir William Blackstone,
> 1870

◀ During an 1870 House of Commons debate about the enfranchisement of women, British politician Sir Charles Dilke (1843-1911) quotes influential British judge Sir William Blackstone (1723-1780) on the matter of voting. Blackstone grouped women with insane people, children, and criminals. Dilke himself supported voting rights for women.

▼ Proceedings in the all-male British Parliament in the mid-1800s. The first woman to serve in the House of Commons was U.S.-born Viscountess Nancy Astor (1879-1964), elected in 1919.

2

3

In the case of election to public trusts, it is the business of constitutional law to surround the right of suffrage with all needful securities and limitations; but whatever securities are sufficient in the case of the male sex, no others need be required in the case of women. Under whatever conditions, and within whatever limits, men are admitted to the suffrage, there is not a shadow of justification for not admitting women under the same.

John Stuart Mill,
The Subjection of Women (1869)

▲ A passage from John Stuart Mill's book *The Subjection of Women* (1869) argues that women should be permitted to vote in public elections on the same terms as men. Mill was a *utilitarian* philosopher who believed that the ultimate goal of public policy should be to promote the general happiness. He believed that giving women equal rights was a step toward this goal.

▶ An illustration from 1893 shows women observing proceedings in the House of Commons from behind a metal grille. The grille was removed in 1917, just two years before Lady Astor took her seat in the House of Commons. Today, there are nearly 150 women in the British House of Commons. However, they still make up less than one-fourth of the entire House.

4

The real question is, whether it is right and *expedient* [advantageous] that one half of the human race should pass through life in a state of forced subordination to the other half.

Harriet Taylor Mill, "The Enfranchisement of Women" (1851)

▲ Harriet Taylor Mill's article "The Enfranchisement of Women" appeared in the British periodical the *Westminster Review* in 1851. James Mill (1773-1836), John Stuart Mill's father, cofounded the utilitarian journal in 1823.

5

NOW YOU KNOW

- John Stuart Mill and Harriet Taylor Mill supported women's suffrage in the United Kingdom.
- John Stuart Mill tried to amend British law to allow women with property to vote.
- No woman had served in the House of Commons until Lady Astor was elected in 1919.

Women's Movement in Britain

A MOVEMENT TO SUPPORT WOMEN'S RIGHTS BEGAN IN THE UNITED KINGDOM in the 1850's. Unlike Chartism, which was a mass movement, the women's rights movement remained small and largely middle-class. Women who organized petitions and spoke at public meetings in support of women's rights drew great disapproval from conservative society. Women's rights supporters wanted to reform marriage and property laws and improve education and working conditions for women. They considered suffrage to be a vital means of giving women a voice in government and overturning laws that discriminated against them. Despite their respectable image, female reformers met great resistance.

1

The Queen is most anxious to enlist everyone who can speak or write or join in checking this mad, wicked folly of "Women's Rights" with all their attendant [accompanying] horrors, on which her poor feeble [weak] sex is bent, forgetting any sense of womanly feeling and propriety [proper behavior].

Queen Victoria of the
United Kingdom, 1870

◀ In a letter to her private secretary, Theodore Martin, dated May 29, 1870, Queen Victoria (1819-1901) expresses her opinion about the British women's rights movement that was emerging. Although Victoria herself was a powerful woman who ruled an empire, she strongly opposed women's rights. Victoria viewed women's suffrage as a challenge to the existing social order and as being against women's nature.

2

▶ Women's suffrage organizations in the United Kingdom produced many magazines and newspapers that dealt with their cause, including *The Common Cause, The Suffragist, The Vote, Votes for Women, The Woman's Journal, The Woman's Journal and Suffrage News, The Woman's Tribune,* and *Women's Suffrage Journal.*

▶ In April 1866, British political leader Benjamin Disraeli (1804-1881) defended women's suffrage in a speech delivered to the House of Commons. The speech concerned the Reform Act of 1867, which gave the vote to many city workers and small farmers in the United Kingdom. However, the act did not extend suffrage to women. In his speech, Disraeli mentions the fact that Britain's head of state at the time was a woman—Queen Victoria. (The *peeresses* Disraeli mentions are female members of the British nobility.)

I say that in a country governed by a woman— where you allow women to form part of the estate of the realm—peeresses in their own right, for example—where you allow a woman not only to hold land, but to be a lady of the manor and hold legal courts and oversee the poor—I do not see, where she has so much to do with the State and Church, on what reasons, if you come to right, she has not the right to vote.

Benjamin Disraeli, 1866

◀ Lydia Becker (1827-1890) was a leading campaigner for women's suffrage. In 1867, Becker helped organize the Manchester National Society for Women's Suffrage, one of the first British organizations dedicated to securing the vote for women. Other suffragist societies soon were created. Becker founded and edited the *Women's Suffrage Journal*. She also was active in *lobbying* Parliament—that is, working to influence the decisions of members of Parliament.

NOW YOU KNOW

• The British women's rights movement of the mid-1800's was small and primarily middle-class.

• Queen Victoria opposed women's suffrage and the women's rights movement in general.

• Lydia Becker was a leader of the women's suffrage movement in the 1800's.

Temperance and Suffrage

IN THE LATE 1800'S, THE UNITED STATES WAS EXPANDING WESTWARD and rapidly becoming industrialized. Immigrants were pouring into growing American cities. More girls and women were attending American schools and colleges than ever before. But life for most women in the United States was difficult and, unlike men, women could not vote. More significant than the women's suffrage movement was *temperance,* the campaign to reduce or eliminate the use of alcoholic beverages. The temperance movement was led mostly by women, many of whom also advocated women's suffrage.

▶ American educator and social reformer Frances Willard (1839-1898) addresses a convention of the Woman's Christian Temperance Union (WCTU) in Denver, Colorado, in 1892. Willard was president of the WCTU from 1879 until her death. In 1890, the WCTU had 150,000 members, while the National American Woman Suffrage Association (NAWSA) had only about 13,000. Willard expanded the scope of the WCTU to deal with issues beyond temperance, such as women's suffrage. She argued that women should seek the vote to obtain physical security, especially against abusive and alcoholic husbands.

1

What lies at the root of everything? Give us the vote, that we may be recognised as if we were capable citizens. Give us the vote, that we may help in purifying politics. . . . Give us the vote, in order that we may use it, and in using it exercise ourselves in the discharge [performing] of responsible duties, in the administration of affairs which form so large a part of the realms of most men.

Frances Willard, 1892

2

The black man had the right of suffrage *conferred upon* [given to] him without his asking for it, and now an attempt is made to force it upon the red man in direct opposition to his wishes, while women citizens, already members of the nation . . . are denied its exercise.

Matilda Joslyn Gage, 1878

◀ Matilda Joslyn Gage (1826-1898), an early leader of the women's rights movement, compares the legal rights of black men, Native American men, and women in an article titled "Indian Citizenship." The article was published in 1878 in *The National Citizen and Ballot Box,* the newspaper of the National Woman Suffrage Association. Gage left the NWSA after it merged with the American Woman Suffrage Association in 1890. The American Woman Suffrage Association was influenced by the WCTU, and Gage disagreed with the conservative religious leanings of the temperance group. She went on to form the Woman's National Liberal Union, which viewed religion as something that oppressed women.

3

▲ Members of the WCTU marched on Washington D.C., in 1909 to present the U.S. government with a petition supporting *prohibition*. Prohibition refers to laws designed to stop people from brewing, purchasing, and consuming alcoholic beverages. From 1920 to 1933, the U.S. Constitution included a prohibition amendment. Women were the backbone of the temperance movement, which was linked closely with the campaign for women's suffrage.

NOW YOU KNOW

- The temperance movement was much larger than the women's suffrage movement in the United States in the late 1800's.
- The temperance movement mobilized support for women's suffrage.
- Frances Willard and Matilda Joslyn Gage were leading American woman suffragists.

Pioneering New Zealand

IN 1893, THE BRITISH COLONY OF NEW ZEALAND GRANTED WOMEN THE VOTE in parliamentary elections. At that time, New Zealand's parliament was a two-house General Assembly that consisted of the colonial governor, an elected House of Representatives, and a Legislative Council appointed by the governor. Although New Zealand was small and far from Europe and North America, women's rights advocates there were quite aware of the American and European debates taking place about women's role in society. The Women's Franchise Leagues were established in 1892 to secure the vote for New Zealand women. The leagues obtained their goal throughout the colony on Sept. 19, 1893, when Governor David Boyle, Lord Glasgow (1833-1915), signed the Electoral Bill, giving women suffrage.

1

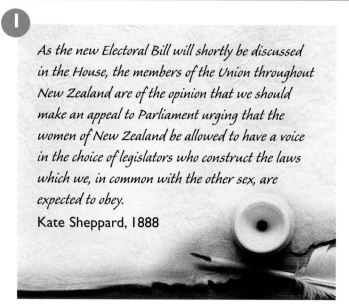

As the new Electoral Bill will shortly be discussed in the House, the members of the Union throughout New Zealand are of the opinion that we should make an appeal to Parliament urging that the women of New Zealand be allowed to have a voice in the choice of legislators who construct the laws which we, in common with the other sex, are expected to obey.

Kate Sheppard, 1888

▲ A letter written in 1888 by the New Zealand suffragist Kate Sheppard (1847-1934) to Sir John Hall (1824-1907), a leading member of the New Zealand parliament. Several bills for women's suffrage proposed from 1878 to 1892 failed to pass.

▶ A petition in support of women's suffrage, organized by Kate Sheppard in 1893, contained more than 30,000 signatures. When the petition was presented to the New Zealand Parliament, Sir John Hall unrolled the huge document down the middle aisle of the House of Representatives debating chamber. Today, the petition is on display at Archives New Zealand, in Wellington.

2

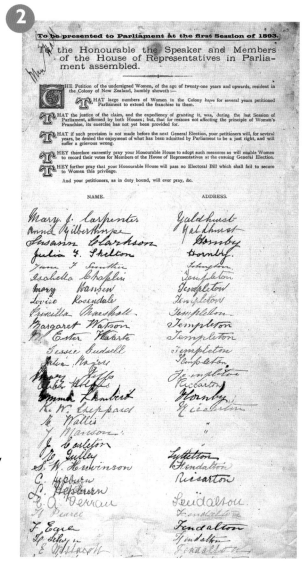

3

▶ "The Glorious 19th," a poem written by David Will M. Burn, celebrates New Zealand women getting the vote. It also expresses a sense of pride in New Zealand for leading the nations of the world in granting women suffrage. The poem appeared in the *North Otago Times* newspaper on Sept. 21, 1893.

THE GLORIOUS 19TH

A trumpet note of Victory,
Rings out across the night,
Now mellowing in the hollows,
Now pealing from the height;
"Ye have the vote!"—O God be praised,
Another step is won
On the golden Stair of Progress
That leadeth to the Sun. . . .

New Zealand, O my country,
I thrill with pride the day,
To think where Nations pause and shrink
Again thou lead'st the way! . . .

David Will M. Burn, 1893

4

◀ New Zealand women vote in an election in 1899. Although women had the right to vote, they could not stand for election to the New Zealand legislature until 1919.

NOW YOU KNOW

- New Zealand granted women the right to vote in 1893.
- Kate Sheppard was a leading campaigner for women's suffrage in New Zealand.
- Women could not run for the New Zealand legislature until 1919.

Australia

AUSTRALIA WAS NOT FAR BEHIND NEW ZEALAND IN GRANTING WOMEN THE VOTE. When Australian women began campaigning for suffrage, Australia was not yet a unified country. It consisted of six colonies, each with its own laws. The suffragists' first victory occurred in South Australia, which in 1894 granted women over the age of 21 the right to vote. Western Australia followed suit in 1899. In 1901, the six Australian colonies joined together to form the Commonwealth of Australia. One year later, in 1902, the young Australian Parliament gave women the right to vote in federal elections, even if they could not yet vote in state elections. The new legislation also gave women the right to run for Parliament. Australian Aborigines were not granted suffrage in federal elections until 1962.

1

Here in New South Wales every man may vote, let his character be bad, his judgment *purchasable* [buyable], and his intellect of the weakest; but an honourable, thoughtful and good woman may be laughed at by such men, they can carry what laws they please in spite of her.

Louisa Lawson,
Dawn, July 1889

◀ Australian editor and publisher Louisa Lawson (1848-1920) comments on the unjustness of voting laws in her women's journal *Dawn* in 1889. Lawson was a working-class woman who founded *Dawn* in 1888 as a periodical "edited, printed and published by women." *Dawn* was a leading voice for women's rights in education, marriage, suffrage, and work. Despite financial problems, Lawson kept publishing the journal until 1905, when most Australian women could vote in state elections.

▶ A typical suffragist advertisement in the *Sydney Morning Herald* of July 31, 1901, urges men not to vote for political candidates who oppose women's suffrage. The Women's Suffrage League sponsored the advertisement. Women in New South Wales gained the right to vote in state elections in 1902. Tasmania and Queensland granted women suffrage in 1903 and 1905, respectively. Victoria was the last state to give women the vote, in 1908.

2

WOMANHOOD SUFFRAGE LEAGUE
ELECTORS OF NEW SOUTH WALES
VOTE FOR NO MAN
Who is AGAINST THE
ENFRANCHISEMENT OF WOMEN
The interests of Women and Children
Cannot be looked after by men alone
Only more than one class can look
after the interests of another class.

Sydney Morning Herald,
July 31, 1901

◀ Vida Goldstein (1869-1949) was one of the most active leaders of the campaign for women's suffrage in Victoria. She traveled widely, promoting women's rights, in Australia and overseas. Goldstein was the first Australian woman to run for the Australian federal Senate, in 1903. Although she was defeated, she received more than 50,000 votes.

NOW YOU KNOW

- In 1902, Australia's federal Parliament granted women suffrage in federal elections.
- By 1908, women could vote in both federal and state elections throughout Australia.
- Louisa Lawson and Vida Goldstein were leaders in the fight for women's suffrage in Australia.

First European Victories

FINLAND WAS THE FIRST REGION IN EUROPE TO GRANT WOMEN THE VOTE on the same terms as men. In 1809, Russia gained control of Finland from Sweden. Finland had some self-government under Russia, but in the late 1800's, many Finnish men and women called for more rights or even independence. When political revolution swept across Russia in 1905, the Finns demanded democratic reforms, including a new parliament and universal suffrage. A law approved in Finland on May 29, 1906, allowed for men and women over 24 years of age to vote and run for election in a new Finnish parliament. In March 1907, 19 women representatives were elected to the new parliament. Since then, Finns have elected many women to their parliament, called the Eduskunta.

▶ Alexandra Gripenberg (1857-1913), a leading Finnish campaigner for women's rights, writes in *The Englishwoman's Review* about her countrywomen gaining the vote in 1906. Gripenberg traveled to the United Kingdom and the United States to study the women's movements there and draw lessons for her own country. She was one of 19 women elected to Finland's parliament in 1907.

▲ A woman casts her ballot in Finland's 1907 parliamentary election.

The miracle has happened! On May the 29th the Finnish *Diet* [parliament] agreed to an Imperial proposal from the Czar concerning changes in the constitution of Finland, which changes also include political suffrage and eligibility to the Diet for Women, married and unmarried, on the same conditions as for men. . . . the constitution committee in the Diet recommended Women's Suffrage and eligibility for the following reasons: the women in Finland get now-a-days exactly the same education as men, even in the same schools as men, since education has been adopted in wide circles. Women are in our time employed side by side with men in different lines of work. . . . there is no reason to fear that women would not use their suffrage and fulfil their duties as citizens as well as men. Finally, the women themselves have shown a strong desire to get the suffrage.

Alexandra Gripenberg, "The Great Victory in Finland," 1906

3

The women are proud of what they said, for they told your England that never in Norway had political life been so moral or so clean and that never had the country been in so fine a condition. . . . They told them that the women had not only surprised the men—they had astonished themselves as they had not guessed till they got political power how much good they could do with that power.

Marta Sandal Bramsen, 1913

◀ The *Morning Albertan* of Feb. 21, 1913, printed an address delivered by Norwegian concert singer Marta Sandal Bramsen (1878-1931) to the Canadian Women's Club. In her address, Bramsen comments on reports that English politicians asked Norwegians about the effect of women's suffrage in Norway. Norway's parliament granted women the right to vote and run in national elections in 1913. Women in Denmark and Iceland gained the vote in 1915. Sweden granted women suffrage in 1921.

▶ Norwegian women participate in an international suffrage parade in the early 1900's. A male supporter of women's suffrage carries the Norwegian flag.

4

NOW YOU KNOW

- In 1906, Finland became the first European region to grant women suffrage on the same terms as men.
- Alexandra Gripenberg was a leading women's rights campaigner in Finland.
- Women in Norway, Denmark, Iceland, and Sweden gained the vote between 1913 and 1919.

Early Militancy in Britain

THE TERM "FEMINIST" WAS COINED IN 1894 to describe people who supported women's rights. The 1890's saw a renewed energy in and commitment to the suffragist cause in Britain. In 1897, the scattered suffrage societies in the United Kingdom combined to form the National Union of Women's Suffrage Societies (NUWSS), which sought to secure women's suffrage by lobbying Parliament. Despite the new organization's best efforts, no women's suffrage bill was proposed in Parliament. A breakaway group called the Women's Social and Political Union (WSPU) was founded in 1903. The WSPU was led by the *charismatic* (fascinating) Emmeline Pankhurst (1858-1928) and her daughters Christabel (1880-1958) and Sylvia (1882-1960). Its *militant* (aggressive) methods brought attention to the struggle for women's suffrage.

1

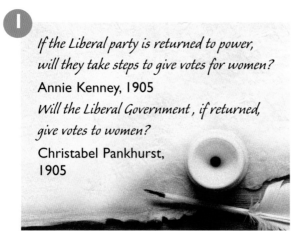

If the Liberal party is returned to power, will they take steps to give votes for women?
Annie Kenney, 1905

Will the Liberal Government , if returned, give votes to women?
Christabel Pankhurst, 1905

◄ British suffragists Annie Kenney (1879-1953) and Christabel Pankhurst stood up and questioned Liberal politicians at a Liberal Party meeting in Manchester on Oct. 13, 1905. The women also submitted their question in writing. They did not receive an answer to their query, but persisted in demanding one. The meeting ended in confusion, and the police were called. Christabel Pankhurst spat at a policeman and was arrested for assault. Annie Kenney was arrested for creating an obstruction in the street. They were the first British suffragists arrested for the cause.

▼ An admission ticket to a demonstration organized by the WSPU for June 21, 1908. The event, held in London, attracted more 250,000 suffragists from all over Britain. The ticket was printed in the suffragist color scheme of purple, white, and green.

2

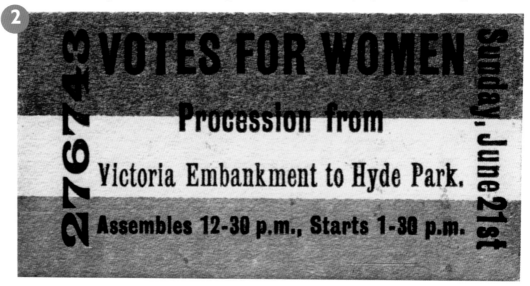

VOTES FOR WOMEN
Procession from
Victoria Embankment to Hyde Park.
Assembles 12-30 p.m., Starts 1-30 p.m.
27 6743
Sunday, June 21st

▶ In an open letter to her fellow suffragists, Millicent Garrett Fawcett (1847-1929) warns against condemning militant tactics. Fawcett became president of the NUWSS in 1897. She promoted change through such means as supporting sympathetic legislators and political parties in Parliament. The NUWSS had about 400 member societies by 1913. Although it did not always approve of the WSPU's militant methods, its members took part in suffragist marches and meetings in huge numbers.

3

We have conducted ourselves with perfect propriety in our middle-class way, and have got nothing for our pains. A new element has come on the scene—working women. They are conducting the campaign in their own way. Their way is not our way; it is possible it may be a better way than ours. Let me counsel all friends of women's suffrage not to denounce the flag waving women who ask questions about suffrage at meetings, even at the risk of rough handling and jeers. It is proving to men what many have not realised—that women are in earnest.

Millicent Garrett Fawcett, open letter to suffrage movement, January 1906

4

◀ Emmeline and Christabel Pankhurst wearing prison uniforms. Emmeline and her daughters regularly tried to get themselves arrested and imprisoned. By presenting themselves as *martyrs* (people who suffer for their beliefs), they attempted to arouse sympathy and support, including financial support. In 1913, Emmeline was sentenced to three years imprisonment. However, she was released from jail after several months.

NOW YOU KNOW

- The 1890's saw a renewal of the women's suffrage movement in the United Kingdom.
- The NUWSS united many scattered suffragist groups in 1897.
- The WSPU, established in 1903, used somewhat militant methods to fight for women's suffrage.

Militant Suffragettes

A NEW WORD, *SUFFRAGETTE*, WAS INVENTED IN 1906. The term *suffragist* had been applied to both women and men. But *suffragette* referred specifically to those women who were prepared to take direct militant action to support their cause. Eventually, many nonmilitant woman suffragists also applied the term *suffragette* to themselves. From 1906 to 1914, British suffragettes deliberately courted arrest through such acts as interrupting public meetings, smashing windows, and damaging public property. The police often treated these women with great brutality. In seven years, they put more than a thousand suffragettes in jail.

▶ A song sung by suffragettes who attended the "Women's Parliament" of Feb. 13, 1907. On that day, hundreds of women met in London and passed a resolution condemning the omission of suffrage in the King's Speech made the previous day. The King's Speech is an address delivered at the start of a session of Parliament. The women tried to deliver their resolution to the prime minister, but mounted police prevented them from entering Parliament. The suffragettes scuffled with the police and dozens of them were arrested.

1

Rise up, women! for the fight is hard and long;
Rise in thousands, singing loud a battle song.
Right is might, and in its strength we shall be strong,
And the Cause goes marching on. . . .

Theodora Mills

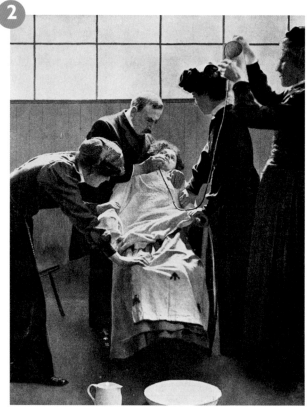

▶ A British suffragette is force-fed at Holloway prison in London. Prison authorities force-fed suffragists on hunger strikes through a tube inserted into the nose or mouth. In *My Own Story* (1914), Emmeline Pankhurst wrote about force-feeding: "Holloway became a place of horror and torment. Sickening scenes of violence took place almost every hour of the day, as the doctors went from cell to cell performing their hideous office. One of the men did his work in such brutal fashion that the very sight of him provoked cries of horror and anguish. I shall never while I live forget the suffering I experienced during the days when those cries were ringing in my ears." Pankhurst herself was imprisoned for suffragist activities.

▶ In a speech called "Freedom or Death," delivered in Hartford, Connecticut, on Nov. 13, 1913, Emmeline Pankhurst used the example of two hungry babies to make her point. She compared militant suffragettes to a hungry baby who makes a lot of fuss and, as a result, gets what it wants.

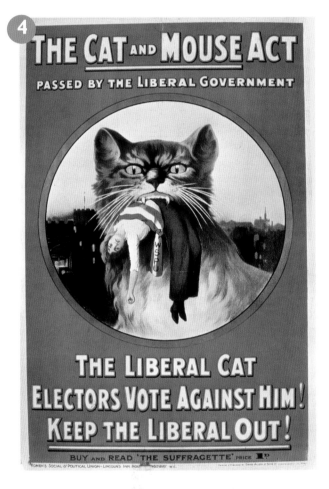

You have two babies very hungry and wanting to be fed. One baby is a patient baby, and waits indefinitely until its mother is ready to feed it. The other baby is an impatient baby and cries lustily [strongly], screams and kicks and makes everybody unpleasant until it is fed. Well, we know perfectly well which baby is attended to first. That is the whole history of politics. You have to make more noise than anybody else, you have to make yourself more obtrusive [pushy] than anybody else, you have to fill all the papers more than anybody else, in fact you have to be there all the time and see that they do not snow you under, if you are really going to get your reform realised.

Emmeline Pankhurst,
"Freedom or Death,"
1913

◀ A poster discourages British voters from supporting the Liberals, who passed the Prisoners' Temporary Discharge for Ill-Health Act of 1913, popularly called the Cat and Mouse Act. Beginning in July 1909, some imprisoned suffragettes went on hunger strikes. The Cat and Mouse Act allowed the government to release prisoners weakened by hunger strike, then rearrest them after they had recovered.

NOW YOU KNOW

- The term *suffragette* was applied to militant woman suffragists beginning in 1906.
- Many suffragettes were arrested and imprisoned for their aggressive activities.
- The Cat and Mouse Act allowed the government to release and rearrest prisoners weakened by hunger strike.

Slow Progress in the U.S.

BY 1900, IT SEEMED TO AMERICAN SUFFRAGISTS that things finally were going their way. Four states had enfranchised women in the 1890's: Wyoming in 1890, Colorado in 1893, and Idaho and Utah in 1896. Despite huge efforts by suffragists, no further progress was made until 1910, when the state of Washington gave women the vote. A year later, California followed suit. By 1916, five more states had fully enfranchised women, either through a *referendum* (direct vote by the people) or legislation. Still, progress was slow, and many suffragists began to look to the methods used by militant suffragettes in the United Kingdom. About 1900, the first generation of woman suffragists began to be replaced with a second, younger generation.

1

> We little dreamed when we began this contest . . . that half a century later we would be compelled [forced] to leave the finish of the battle to another generation of women. But our hearts are filled with joy to know that they enter upon this task equipped with a college education, with business experience, with the freely admitted right to speak in public—all of which were denied to women fifty years ago.
>
> Susan B. Anthony, 1902

◀ A letter written by Susan B. Anthony to Elizabeth Cady Stanton toward the end of both women's lives details how younger women with new campaigning skills were succeeding the original suffragists. Anthony and Stanton had remained at the helm of the women's suffrage movement for half a century and earned tremendous respect for their efforts. Stanton died in 1902 and Anthony died in 1906.

▶ Carrie Chapman Catt (1859-1947) poses as the new president of NAWSA in 1900. Stanton, who chose Catt as president, believed that Catt's organizational and campaigning skills would give the aging suffrage movement greater momentum. Catt served as president of the organization from 1900 to 1904 and from 1915 to 1920, when the 19th Amendment to the U.S. Constitution gave women the right to vote.

2

▶ In a 1902 speech to an NAWSA convention, Carrie Chapman Catt speaks about the challenges still facing the suffragists. Catt thought that the process of gaining suffrage one state at a time was too slow. Despite hundreds of campaigns to get state legislatures to pass women's suffrage amendments, women in many states still could not vote. Catt believed that the only way to win the vote for women was through an act of the U.S. Congress.

3

In the United States, at least, we need no longer to argue women's intellectual, moral and physical qualifications with the intelligent. The Reason of the best of our citizens has long been convinced. The justice of our argument has been admitted, but sex prejudice is far from conquered.

Carrie Chapman Catt, 1902

4

▲ Police escort demonstrators for women's suffrage from New York City Hall in 1908. Even when demonstrating, suffragists dressed with great care to show that they were respectable women.

NOW YOU KNOW

- A second generation of suffragists began to take over the leadership of the U.S. women's suffrage movement in the early 1900's.

- By 1916, women in 11 U.S. states had full voting rights.

- Carrie Chapman Catt sought women's suffrage through an act of the U.S. Congress.

International Links

B Y THE OUTBREAK OF WORLD WAR I (1914-1918), the women's suffrage movement was truly international. Faster transportation and communication systems made it easier for suffragists to exchange ideas and to organize. Women in the United Kingdom and the United States followed with interest and envy the victories won by women in New Zealand and Australia. News of Canadian and European suffragists' struggles were reported in various suffragist publications. The most effective means of gaining attention and spreading suffragist ideas, however, was the public meeting. Many women became excellent speakers, despite the fact that their audiences often were hostile.

▶ Writing in a suffragist journal in 1911, British activist Sylvia Pankhurst comments on the effects of the British and American suffrage campaigns on each other. Sylvia's mother, Emmeline, in 1909 visited the United States on a speaking tour that attracted huge, enthusiastic crowds. The Pankhursts were in great demand as speakers.

▼ One of the largest suffragette demonstrations took place in London in June 1911, with delegations from many countries. One delegation came from Australia, where women had had federal voting rights since 1902. The Australian delegation included Margaret Fisher, the prime minister's wife; Emily McGowen, the New South Wales premier's wife; and Vida Goldstein, a famous suffragist from Victoria.

All over America the suffragists declare that they have gained hope and inspiration from our great British movement. In the early days of our long struggle, it was we who drew inspiration from them. Our movements act and react on each other. We and the world have much to gain from our joint effort.

Sylvia Pankhurst, 1911

FROM PRISON

TO CITIZENSHIP

SUFFRAGETTE PROCESSION JUNE 17, 1911.

3

On a cloud covered day as well as a bright

Towards the future we raise our *standard* [flag]

Forward through the clouds and mist

Towards the light of a new day.

International Woman
Suffrage Alliance banner

◀ A verse printed on the back of a banner of the International Woman Suffrage Alliance (IWSA). The IWSA was founded in 1902 as the International Alliance of Women for Suffrage and Legal Citizenship. Women from 11 countries attended the founding meeting in Washington, D.C. Carrie Chapman Catt served as president of the IWSA from 1904-1923. The organization's newly created banner was presented to Catt at a congress in Stockholm, Sweden, in 1911. The front of the banner had a sunburst design. Since 1926, the group has been named the International Alliance of Women.

▶ An American poster made during World War I contrasts U.S. women's disenfranchisement with the voting of *aliens* (noncitizens). The fine print says that in some states, aliens who had declared their intention to become naturalized citizens could vote. Some, however, then claimed exemption from the draft for military service.

4

American Women

are urged to work in

Munition Plants
Railway Yards
Land Armies
Elevators
Trolley Cars
Ambulance Driving
Red Cross
Nursing, Etc.

BUT in most States They are **NOT** trusted To Vote

Enemy Aliens

are NOT trusted to work in

Munition Plants
Nor in many other war activities

BUT They ARE TRUSTED To Vote

In Eight States Foreigners Vote on First Papers. In Nebraska in one County alone 785 men Claimed Exemption from the Draft because they were "Enemy Aliens," But Admitted They Had Voted for years.

FOR THE HOME DEFENSE

Support those Candidates for the Legislature Who Stand for Woman Suffrage

NOW YOU KNOW

- By the first decade of the 1900's, suffragists in different countries had formed significant connections.
- Public meetings were an effective way for suffragists to communicate, and many suffragists became talented speakers.
- Women from 11 nations founded the IWSA in 1902 in Washington, D.C.

World War I

THE OUTBREAK OF WORLD WAR I IN AUGUST 1914 had an immediate impact on women's rights groups in the warring nations. Some suffragists tried to rebuild links between enemy countries by holding a peace conference at The Hague, the seat of the government of the neutral Netherlands, in 1915. But most women's suffrage groups suspended their suffragist activities to refocus their energies on the war effort. Many suffragists were motivated by genuine patriotism. Many also believed that taking part in the war effort would help advance women's rights. In the United Kingdom, both the militant WSPU and the more moderate NUWSS supported the war.

1

It is obvious that even the most vigorous militancy of the WSPU is for the time being rendered less effective by contrast with the infinitely greater violence done in the present war not to mere property and economic prosperity alone, but to human life. . . . Under all the circumstances it has been decided to economise the Union's energies and activities by a temporary suspension of activities. . . . we ardently desire that our country should be victorious.

Emmeline Pankhurst, 1914

◀ A letter dated Aug. 13, 1914, from Emmeline Pankhurst to members of the WSPU explains her decision to suspend the group's suffragist activities. The British government had agreed to release all imprisoned suffragettes. In return, Pankhurst agreed to call off all WSPU activities and devote her energies to the war effort. But she failed to consult with other WSPU members before making this decision, and many of them disagreed with her.

2

THE WOMAN'S LAND ARMY of AMERICA

WOMEN *enlist now and help the* FARMER FIGHT THE FOOD FAMINE

APPLY: National Office, 19 West 44th Street
New York State Office, 303 Fifth Avenue
OR: Nearest U. S. Employment Bureau office

▶ A recruitment poster urges U.S. women to join the Women's Land Army of America (WLAA) during World War I. The WLAA was established by various women's organizations, including suffragist organizations, to replace male farmworkers who had gone off to war. The tens of thousands of women, called "farmerettes," who joined the WLAA were for the most part urban women who had never done farm work before. The WLAA was modeled on a similar organization in the United Kingdom.

▶ Sylvia Pankhurst explains her opposition to World War I in her book *The Home Front: A Mirror to Life in England During the World War* (1932). Sylvia was expelled from the WSPU in January 1914 because of her socialist views. She then worked with the East London Federation of Suffragettes, later renamed the Workers' Suffrage Federation (WSF), to help working-class women and, later, to oppose the war.

3

I could not give my name to aid the slaughter in this war, fought on both sides for grossly material ends, which did not justify the sacrifice of a single mother's son. Clearly I must continue to oppose it, and expose it, to all whom I could reach with voice or pen.

Sylvia Pankhurst,
The Home Front (1932)

▼ British women work on an assembly line in a *munitions* (military supplies) factory during World War I. During the war, women were needed to fill jobs previously held only by men.

4

NOW YOU KNOW

- Most suffragist organizations suspended their activities during World War I.
- Some suffragists believed that their participation in the war effort would further women's rights.
- During World War I, many women replaced fighting men in agricultural and industrial jobs, proving that they were neither weak nor incapable.

Canada

IKE AUSTRALIAN AND AMERICAN WOMEN, Canadian women had to win the vote at both local and national levels. In January 1916, Manitoba became the first province to give women suffrage in provincial elections. Saskatchewan and Alberta granted women suffrage later in 1916. Most other provinces followed suit over the next few years. Quebec was the last province to grant women suffrage, in 1940. In 1917, during World War I, the federal government passed the Military Voters Act, which gave all people in the military, including women, the vote in federal elections. The government also passed the War-time Elections Act, which allowed female relatives of military men to vote in federal elections. Suffragists protested vigorously that the act was unfair. The Canada Elections Act of 1918 finally gave all Canadian women over the age of 21 the right to vote in federal elections, whether or not they could vote in provincial elections at that time.

1

The trouble is that if men start to vote, they will vote too much. Politics unsettles men, and unsettled men means unsettled bills, broken furniture, broken vows and—divorce. . . . If men were to get into the habit of voting—who knows what might happen—it's hard enough to keep them home now. History is full of unhappy examples of men in public life—Nero, Herod, King John . . .

The Women's Parliament (1914)

◀ On Jan. 28, 1914, Canadian suffragist Nellie McClung (1873-1951) and other members of the Manitoba Political Equality League staged a play titled *The Women's Parliament* at the Walker Theatre in Winnipeg. The play, which ridiculed Manitoba Premier Sir Rodmond Roblin (1853-1937), was a great success. Roblin had just rejected a bill granting women the vote in provincial elections. The play took his arguments against woman suffrage and applied them to men.

2

▶ Nellie McClung was one of the Famous Five. In 1927, this group of female reformers asked the Supreme Court of Canada to examine the meaning of the word "persons" in the British North America Act, Canada's constitution. In 1928, the Supreme Court decided women were not "persons" and so could not serve in Canada's Senate. The Famous Five appealed to the Judicial Committee of Britain's Privy Council, the highest court of appeal for Canada at that time. In 1929, the Judicial Committee concluded that "the word 'persons' includes both the male and female sex."

▶ In a personal recollection written in 1943, Nova Scotia journalist and suffragist Ella Maud Murray comments on how World War I aided the campaign for women's voting rights in Canada.

▼ Canadian nurses, called "Bluebirds" because they wore bright blue uniforms, vote at a field hospital in France in December 1917. The Bluebirds were the first Canadian women to vote in a federal election. The Military Voters Act gave the vote to military nurses. The War-time Elections Act gave the vote to female relatives of men who were serving or had served in the war. The laws excluded other women, including some who could vote in provincial elections.

At the end it came without struggle in recognition of women's services during the war. Things often work out that way I find. You struggle and struggle to no direct effect, and suddenly in a lull [quiet time] the whole thing snaps into place.

Ella Maud Murray, 1943

NOW YOU KNOW

- Manitoba, Saskatchewan, and Alberta were the first Canadian provinces to grant women suffrage, in 1916.
- In 1918, Canada's federal government gave all women over 21 the right to vote in federal elections.
- Women in Quebec could not vote in provincial elections until 1940.

Success in the United Kingdom

AFTER BRITISH WOMEN CONTRIBUTED SO MUCH TO THE WAR EFFORT, men could no longer claim that they were weak or incapable. Although the main suffrage societies had suspended their public activities during the war, they had continued lobbying Parliament quietly. By the end of World War I, most British politicians agreed that women should have the vote. The Representation of the People Act of 1918 extended suffrage to British women more than 30 years old. British men, however, could vote after they turned 21. Ten years later, Parliament passed the Representation of the People Act of 1928, which finally gave women voting rights on the same terms as men.

1

. . . but they fill our munition factories, they are doing the work which the men who are fighting had to perform before, they have taken their places, they are the servants of the State, and they have aided, in the most effective way, in the prosecution [carrying out] of the War. . . . I say quite frankly that I cannot deny that claim.

Herbert Asquith, 1916

▲ In a speech to Parliament in August 1916, British Prime Minister Herbert Asquith (1852-1928) acknowledges women's contributions in World War I. Asquith served as prime minister from 1908 to 1916. Because he was opposed to women's suffrage during his administration, Asquith became a chief target for militant suffragettes. Asquith later claimed that women's work during the war helped him change his mind about women's right to vote.

▶ A British wartime poster illustrates the importance of women who worked in *munitions* factories during World War I. Munitions are such military supplies as guns, ammunition, and bombs.

2

ON HER THEIR LIVES DEPEND

WOMEN MUNITION WORKERS

Enrol at once

▶ A personal account by Maud Arncliffe Sennett (1862-1936), a British businesswoman and suffragist, describes the difficulty of registering to vote in the December 1918 parliamentary election. The Representation of the People Act of 1918 extended suffrage to about 8.5 million women. Although suffrage societies helped eligible women register to vote, the process could be difficult and disheartening.

3

Mrs Smith and I spent all morning trying to find the place to vote (i.e. to register) without success. Everyone we asked was so nasty and I quite understand how beastly it must have been to have had that wall of insulting prejudice against one in every turn if they are like this now that it is won!

Maud Arncliffe Sennett, 1918

4

◀ An illustration by the Italian artist Fortunino Matania (1881-1963) depicts a British woman casting her ballot in the general election of Dec. 14, 1918. The election marked the first time that British women could vote for their representatives in Parliament. However, only women over 30 years of age could vote.

NOW YOU KNOW

- Women's contributions in World War I helped convince the British government to extend voting rights to women.
- The Representation of the People Act of 1918 gave the vote to British women over 30.
- It was not until 1928 that Parliament granted women suffrage on the same terms as men.

Ireland

AT THE BEGINNING OF THE 1900's, IRELAND WAS PART OF THE UNITED KINGDOM of Great Britain and Ireland. Like British women, Irish women had no voting rights in national elections. The first women's suffrage organizations in Ireland were established in the 1870's. The most important of these groups took the name Irish Women's Suffrage and Local Government Association (IWSLGA) in 1901. A more militant group, the Irish Women's Franchise League, was founded in 1908. Some, but not all, Irish suffragettes also supported Irish independence from Britain. In 1918, women over 30 gained the vote in Ireland and other parts of the United Kingdom. In 1921, most of Ireland became a *dominion* (self-governing country) of the British Commonwealth. The constitution of the new government of the dominion, called the Irish Free State, granted suffrage to women and men aged 21 years and older in 1922.

▶ The motto of the *Irish Citizen* newspaper advocated equal civic rights and duties for women and men. The Irish Women's Franchise League established the newspaper in 1912 to educate the public and produce *propaganda* for women's suffrage in Ireland. Propaganda refers to a plan for spreading certain opinions or beliefs.

1

For Men and Women Equally
The Rights of Citizenship
From Men and Women equally
The Duties of Citizenship

motto of the *Irish Citizen*

▼ The Easter Rising of April 1916, an armed rebellion against British rule in Ireland, left parts of Dublin badly damaged. British troops crushed the rebellion after about a week and executed its leaders.

2

3

> The Irish Republic is entitled to, and hereby claims, the allegiance of every Irishman and Irishwoman. The Republic government guarantees religious and civil liberty, equal rights and equal opportunity to all its citizens and declares its resolve to pursue the happiness and prosperity of the whole nation and of all its parts, cherishing all the children of the nation equally . . .
>
> from the Proclamation of the Irish Republic, 1916

◄ Nationalist rebels issued the Proclamation of the Irish Republic during the Easter Rising of 1916. This portion of the proclamation describes an independent Irish government under which all citizens, both men and women, have equal rights and equal opportunities and are valued equally.

4

► Countess Markievicz (1868-1927) was an Irish feminist and nationalist. She joined the Irish nationalist political party Sinn Féin *(shihn fayn)* and took an active part in the Easter Rising of 1916. In 1918, when women over 30 won suffrage in the United Kingdom, Markievicz ran for a seat in the British Parliament and won. She was the only woman to do so. Because she favored Irish independence, she declined to take her seat in the House of Commons. In 1919, Markievicz became minister of labor in the Dáil Éireann *(dawl AIR uhn),* the Irish House of Representatives.

NOW YOU KNOW

- Many Irish suffragists also supported independence for Ireland.
- The Proclamation of the Irish Republic supported equal rights for all Irish citizens.
- The constitution of the Irish Free State gave women suffrage on equal terms with men in 1922.

The Winning Plan

By 1916, the National American Woman Suffrage Association (NAWSA) had 200,000 members, and 11 U.S. states had given women full voting rights in all elections. But working for suffrage state by state was slow and demoralizing. In 1916, NAWSA President Carrie Chapman Catt told suffrage leaders that they needed to change tactics and launched her "Winning Plan." Catt's plan was to lobby federal and state politicians intensely to support a suffrage amendment to the U.S. Constitution. Catt launched a coordinated political campaign, and her Winning Plan worked. By late August 1920, 36 states had agreed to a constitutional amendment granting women suffrage. In 1920, the 19th Amendment to the Constitution extended voting rights to all women citizens of the United States.

1

When the full number of signatures had been *affixed* (added) to the *compact* (agreement) and we filed out of the room, I felt like Moses on the mountain top after the Promised Land had been shown to him and he knew the long years of wandering in the wilderness were soon to end. For the first time I saw our goal as possible of attainment in the near future. But we had to have swift and concerted action from every part of the country. Could we get it? Could we get it?

Maud Wood Park,
Front Door Lobby (1960)

◀ In the book *Front Door Lobby* (1960), American feminist Maud Wood Park (1871-1955) remembers her reaction after Carrie Chapman Catt presented her Winning Plan at an NAWSA convention in Atlantic City, New Jersey, in 1916. Catt invited Park to coordinate efforts to win the support of the U.S. Congress in passing a suffrage amendment. Park's tireless work was a major factor in the 1920 passage of the 19th Amendment to the U.S. Constitution. Park wrote the manuscript for *Front Door Lobby* in the 1920's. It was published in 1960, after her death.

2

▶ In a 1917 account written while she was in jail, suffragist Rose Winslow (d. 1977) describes being force-fed. Not all suffragists agreed with NAWSA's political methods. In 1913, Alice Paul (1885-1977) formed the Congressional Union, and in 1916, she helped form the National Woman's Party (NWP). Both groups used militant tactics. Paul, Winslow, Lucy Burns (1879-1966) and other women associated with the NWP were arrested and imprisoned for such activities as picketing outside the White House. Those who went on hunger strike as a form of protest were brutally force-fed by prison authorities. Rubber tubing was used to force soft food into the women's noses or throats.

Yesterday was a bad day for me in feeding. I was vomiting continually during the process.... Don't let them tell you we take this well. Miss Paul vomits much.... We think of the coming feeding with dread. It is horrible. God knows we don't want women ever to have to do this again.
Rose Winslow, 1917

▲ Victorious suffragists celebrate the ratification of the 19th Amendment to the U.S. Constitution in 1920. The amendment extended the right to vote in U.S. elections to American women who were at least 21 years old.

▶ The 19th Amendment was *proposed* (passed by both houses of Congress and sent to the states for approval) on June 4, 1919. It was *ratified* (approved by enough states) on Aug. 18, 1920.

The right of citizens of the United States to vote should not be denied or *abridged* (taken away) by the United States or by any state on account of sex.

Congress shall have power to enforce this article by appropriate legislation.

The 19th Amendment to the U.S. Constitution, 1920

NOW YOU KNOW

- Carrie Chapman Catt and the NAWSA sought to gain women's suffrage by lobbying lawmakers at the national and state levels.
- The National Woman's Party employed militant tactics like picketing and hunger strikes.
- The 19th Amendment to the U.S. Constitution was ratified on Aug. 18, 1920.

Widespread Victories

WORLD WAR I RESULTED IN MAJOR POLITICAL CHANGES IN EUROPE. Empires were broken up. New nations came into being, and other countries gained independence. Democratic and revolutionary ideas circulated freely. Women's suffrage, which only a few years earlier had been seen as revolutionary, became widely accepted. From 1918 to 1920, women gained the vote in a number of European countries. In Russia, women demanded and got the vote after the February Revolution of 1917 unseated the czar. In Latin America, Ecuador granted women suffrage in 1929, and Brazil, Cuba, and Uruguay followed suit in the early 1930's. Women in the Philippines in 1937 took part in a unique *referendum* (direct vote) to determine whether they would obtain suffrage.

1

We have come here to remind you that women were your faithful comrades in the gigantic struggle for the freedom of the Russian people; that they have also been filling up the prisons, and boldly marched to the galleys. . . . We declare that the Constituent Assembly in which only one half of the population will be represented can in no wise be regarded as expressing the will of the whole people, but only half of it. We want no more promises of good will. We have had enough of them! We demand an efficient and clear answer—that the women will have votes in the Constituent Assembly.

Poliksena Shishkina-Iavein, 1917

◀ In an uncompromising speech delivered to the leaders of Russia's provisional government in March 1917, Russian feminist Poliksena Shishkina-Iavein (1875?-1947?) demands that women be allowed to vote for members of Russia's new Constituent Assembly. Shishkina-Iavein voiced her demand after marching with about 40,000 women to the Tauride Palace in Petrograd (now St. Petersburg), the meeting place of the provisional government. Just days later, Georgi Lvov, the prime minister, committed to including women in Russia's new electoral laws.

▶ Filipino historian and feminist Encarnación Alzona (1895-2001) writes about the orderly character of the women's suffrage movement in the Philippines. When the Philippines became a U.S. commonwealth in 1935, its new constitution did not grant suffrage to women. A special referendum for women only was held on April 30, 1937, to determine whether they should get voting rights. About 90 percent of women who took part in the election voted "yes." In September, the National Assembly approved the results of the referendum.

2

The character of our women forbids them to resort to the militant methods employed by British women, for example. They will wait for the duly constituted authorities to pass the law which will enfranchise them. They have confidence in the *sagacity* [wisdom] of our legislators.

Encarnacíon Alzona, 1930

3

◀ Filipino suffragist Trinidad Fernandez Legarda (1899-1998) as queen of the 1924 Manila Carnival. Legarda was active in the National Federation of Women's Clubs of the Philippines (NFWC), which worked for women's rights, including suffrage. She served as an NFWC board member or adviser during most of the period from 1921 to 1992. She was the organization's president from 1946 to 1952 and served as an editor of its official publication, *Women's Outlook*. Like many other Filipino women, she believed that suffragists should not sacrifice beauty or femininity or rely upon militancy.

4

We believe in our cause but we do not believe that to *attain* [achieve] our end we have to resort to violent and drastic methods which would only reflect upon ourselves. We are of the *conviction* [belief] that good manners and soft words will bring the most difficult things to pass.

Trinidad Fernandez Legarda, 1931

▶ In a 1931 article in *Philippine Magazine,* Trinidad Fernandez Legarda writes about Filipino suffragists' peaceable approach to obtaining voting rights.

NOW YOU KNOW

- Women in a number of European countries were granted suffrage soon after World War I.
- Women in a number of Latin American nations obtained the vote from the late 1920's to the early 1930's.
- A 1937 referendum secured women's suffrage in the Philippines, where many suffragists rejected militant tactics.

India and Pakistan

In the early 1900's, India was part of the British Empire. Small numbers of Indians, including a few women, were allowed to vote in provincial elections. For most women, however, suffrage was much less important than the nationalist struggle for Indian independence. Women participated in marches and nonviolent protests organized by political parties such as the Indian National Congress and the Muslim League. Thousands of women protesters were arrested and imprisoned. In 1947, British and Indian leaders agreed to divide India to create two nations—India and Pakistan—in an effort to end fighting between Hindus and Muslims. Both countries became independent in August 1947. When they wrote their new constitutions, both countries granted universal suffrage to men and women.

▶ In an article published in the newspaper *Young India* on July 21, 1921, Indian political and religious leader Mohandas Gandhi (1869-1948) expresses his support for women's suffrage. Gandhi wanted to improve the treatment of women in Indian society. He argued that giving women suffrage was a vital step toward bettering girls' and women's lives. Gandhi once wrote that witnessing suffragettes protesting in London helped inspire his own nonviolent demonstrations for Indian independence.

▼ Thousands of Indian women took part in such anti-British protests as the 1930 salt march, when protesters marched to the sea to collect salt from seawater. The march was a protest against the Salt Acts, which made it a crime to possess salt not bought from the government.

1

I passionately desire the utmost freedom for our women. I *detest* [hate] child marriages. I shudder to see a child widow, and shiver with rage when a husband just widowed with brutal indifference contracts another marriage. I deplore the criminal *indifference* [lack of care] of parents who keep their daughters utterly ignorant and illiterate and bring them up only for the purpose of marrying them off to some young man of means. Not withstanding all this grief and rage, I realise the difficulty of the problem. Women must have votes and an equal legal status. But the problem does not end there. It only *commences* [starts] at the point when women begin to affect the political deliberations of the nation.

Mohandas Gandhi, 1921

2

3

There could never be an equal partnership where women were not only economically dependent on their male relatives but also dependent on them for citizens' rights.

S. Muthulakshmi Reddi, 1931

◀ S. Muthulakshmi Reddi (1886-1968), an Indian nationalist and feminist, argues for civic rights for Indian women. At the time, only a few Indian women met the property-ownership or income requirements for voting. The British government wanted to allow the wives and widows of men who met such requirements to vote, but other women would still be excluded. Reddi was one of India's first woman physicians and the first woman legislator in India.

4

▶ Indian women in the city of Gorakhpur, Uttar Pradesh, show their voter identity cards as they wait to vote in a national parliamentary election in 2009.

NOW YOU KNOW

- A few Indian women could vote in provincial elections in the early 1900's.
- Gandhi supported women's suffrage as a step toward improving Indian women's lives.
- After India and Pakistan became independent in 1947, their new constitutions granted women suffrage.

Suffrage After World War II

LIKE WORLD WAR I, WORLD WAR II (1939-1945) BROUGHT far-reaching changes to people's lives, even if their countries were not involved in the conflict. The Allied nations fought the war partly to defend democratic values, which included universal suffrage. After the war, well-established women's suffrage movements gained momentum in countries where women had long been fighting for the vote. In other nations, demands for women's suffrage were part of a larger movement for national independence or racial equality after World War II. By 1960, women in most of the nations of Europe, North and South America, and Asia had gained the right to vote.

▶ In an article published in the May 19, 1919, issue of *L'Humanité* newspaper, French feminist Cécile Brunschvicg (1877-1946) writes about French women's lack of voting rights. In 1909, Brunschvicg helped found the Union Française pour le Suffrage des Femmes (French Union for Women's Suffrage). She was also active in the Conseil National des Femmes Françaises (National Council of French Women). As well as women's suffrage, Brunschvicg advocated equal pay and expanded educational opportunities for women; and reform of the French civil code, which treated married women as minors. Frenchwomen were unofficially given the vote in 1944, in a decree issued by General Charles de Gaulle (1890-1970), the leader of the French provisional government in exile. The decree described how the French government would be reestablished after the war. Women first voted in France in April 1945. Brunschvicg lived long enough to be able to vote.

1

> It is humiliating to think that we are French women, daughters of the land of the Revolution, and that in the year of grace 1919, we are still reduced to demanding the rights of women.
>
> Cécile Brunschvicg, 1919

2

> When women have access to the organs of public power, they will remove all stains, errors and vices so deeply rooted here, discrediting and *impairing* [damaging] *conscientious* [upright] citizenship.
>
> Atilia Sánchez, 1944

◀ Quoted in the magazine *Agitación femenina* in 1944, Colombian feminist Atilia Sánchez looks forward to a time when Colombian women will have the power to improve their government. She predicts that when women become involved in government, they will eliminate the problems that undermine good citizenship. Sánchez was a member of the Alianza Femenina de Colombia (Colombian Women's Alliance), one of the organizations that fought for woman suffrage in Colombia. In 1936, an amendment to Colombia's Constitution provided for universal male suffrage, but it did not include women.

▲ Swiss women urge men to vote *ja,* meaning "yes," in a 1971 referendum on women's suffrage. Although Switzerland has a long tradition of democracy, Swiss women gained the vote much later than did most other European women. In a 1957 referendum, 69 percent of male voters opposed women's suffrage. In 1968, Switzerland found that it could not sign the Convention for the Protection of Human Rights and Fundamental Freedoms unless it allowed women certain civil and political rights, including suffrage. In a second referendum, in 1971, Swiss men approved extending suffrage to women in national elections. However, one *canton* (political division) refused to let women stand for election until 1990, when Switzerland's Federal Tribunal ruled that it must do so.

NOW YOU KNOW

- Woman suffrage movements gained new strength after World War II.
- By 1960, women in most countries in Europe, North and South America, and Asia could vote.
- Switzerland granted women suffrage in 1971.

Postcolonial Africa

DURING THE 1800's, EUROPEAN COUNTRIES CONTROLLED MOST OF AFRICA. As women's suffrage spread in Europe in the early and mid-1900's, some women in European colonies also gained voting rights. But such voting restrictions as education, income, and property-ownership requirements limited the number of nonwhite women and men who could vote in these colonies. After World War II, there was increased pressure on European governments to grant their African colonies independence. Between 1950 and 1980, 47 independent African nations were born. The governments of most of these countries initially gave men and women equal voting rights. In practice, however, voting could be problematic. In some African countries, military dictators abolished elections. In others, elections were corrupt.

1

It is interesting that most women witnesses, when asked if they would follow their husbands' instructions when voting replied that they would use their own judgement. . . . Their replies were illuminating. Typical was the reply of a woman of Chake Chake. She said "I will reply 'Yes Sir' to my husband when he wishes me to vote for a certain candidate; this will please him and keep harmony; but I will vote for my own choice, and as the vote is secret my husband will never know."

Report of the Committee on
Extension of the Franchise to
Women, Zanzibar Protectorate, 1959

◀ A government report from 1959 describes the attitude of women in the British protectorate of Zanzibar toward women's suffrage. The committee that produced the report found that there was little opposition to women's suffrage in Zanzibar, even though the island group had a traditional Muslim society. The committee recommended that, like men, women be permitted to vote after turning 21 years of age. Women gained the vote in 1961, shortly before Zanzibar gained independence from the United Kingdom in 1963. In 1964, Zanzibar merged with the former British colony of Tanganyika to form Tanzania.

▶ Algerian women cast ballots in a July 1, 1962, referendum on Algerian independence. Algerians voted overwhelmingly for independence from France. Algeria was formally proclaimed independent by France on July 3, 1962, following a bloody revolution.

2

▶ In an interview from 1978, Kenyan politician Julia Ojiambo describes women's enthusiastic participation in elections in Kenya. Ojiambo became Kenya's first woman Cabinet minister in 1978. During her election campaign, Ojiambo faced strong opposition from her male opponents, who threatened and beat her and her family, nearly killing her husband. All Kenyan women were granted suffrage in 1963, when Kenya became independent from the United Kingdom.

▼ Egyptians cheer outside the presidential mansion in Cairo as President Gamal Abdel Nasser announces the enfranchisement of Egyptian women in 1956.

> The women in Kenya are the voters. They have the biggest vote. They could literally control the election by their wishes. They participate in all the campaigns, rallies and meetings. When it actually comes to the polling date, they'll be there. The men will probably say: "I'll come later." But the women will always vote.
>
> Julia Ojiambo, 1978

NOW YOU KNOW

- During the 1800's, much of Africa was ruled by European countries.
- Many African nations became independent between 1950 and 1980, and most of them granted women suffrage on equal terms with men.
- Military dictators and corruption sometimes have prevented Africans from voting effectively.

South Africa

THE POLITICAL SITUATION IN SOUTH AFRICA DIFFERED SIGNIFICANTLY from the situation in many other African nations. From the 1940's to the 1990's, South Africa's government enforced a rigid policy of racial segregation called *apartheid,* meaning *separateness.* A small white population owned most of the land and wealth and had full political rights. The majority of South Africans—black Africans, Coloureds (people of mixed race), and Asians (mostly Indians)—were poor and had few political rights. Because most people could not vote, there was no way for them to change government policies. It took decades of struggle by the country's nonwhite majority to end apartheid and create a society where everybody was equal under the law. White women won suffrage in 1930, but other women could not vote until 1994.

► At a parliamentary committee meeting in 1926, South African suffragist Aletta Nel offers her opinion about race and woman suffrage in South Africa. The Women's Enfranchisement Association of the Union (WEAU) began campaigning for woman suffrage in the Union of South Africa (now the Republic of South Africa) in 1911, but it was concerned mainly with voting rights for white women. Some male politicians supported suffrage for white women. They believed that white women would support their efforts to change a law that already allowed a small number of black African and Coloured men in one province to vote. White women were granted suffrage in 1930.

1

Question: Do you favour votes for all women, irrespective of colour?

Answer: As a woman, sir, yes . . . but as a South African born person, I feel that it would be wiser if we gave the vote to the European woman only.

The Report of the Select Committee on the Enfranchisement of Women, 1926

2

We declare the following aims:

This organisation is formed for the purpose of uniting women in common action for the removal of all political, legal, economic and social disabilities. We shall strive for women to obtain:
1. The right to vote and to be elected to all State bodies, without restriction or discrimination.

from the Women's Charter, April 17, 1954

◄ At its founding conference in Johannesburg on April 17, 1954, the Federation of South African Women (FSAW) adopted the Women's Charter, which stated a list of its goals, including the right to vote for and be elected to state bodies. The FSAW included members from all of South Africa's racial groups. The organization worked primarily to support the poorest black African women. Black Africans' homes, schools, and health facilities were inferior to those of other racial groups. In addition, black Africans were treated brutally by the police. Disenfranchisement was just one of the many indignities that they had to endure.

▶ South Africa's Constitution, adopted in 1996, grants suffrage to all adults, regardless of race or sex. In 1993, South Africa adopted a temporary constitution that provided for a new government. The new government, under the leadership of President Nelson Mandela, took office in May 1994, following the country's first all-race elections. In 1996, South Africa completed a new constitution. South Africa's Constitutional Assembly adopted the document on Oct. 11, 1996. Most of its provisions took effect in 1997.

3

The Republic of South Africa is one, sovereign, democratic state founded on the following values:

a. Human dignity, the achievement of equality and the advancement of human rights and freedoms.

b. Non-racialism and non-sexism.

c. Supremacy of the constitution and the rule of law.

d. Universal adult suffrage, a national common voters roll, regular elections and a multi-party system of democratic government, to ensure accountability, responsiveness and openness.

Constitution of the Republic of South Africa, 1996

4

◀ South African political leader Albertina Sisulu (1918-) votes in her country's 2009 parliamentary election. Sisulu helped found the Federation of South African Women. She was also a member of the South African Parliament from 1994 to 1999. Sisulu belongs to the African National Congress (ANC), a political party that played a major role in winning political and civil rights for South Africa's blacks and other nonwhites.

NOW YOU KNOW

- White South African women won the right to vote in 1930.
- South Africa's first all-race election was held in 1994.
- South Africa's Constitution, adopted in its complete form in 1996, granted suffrage to men and women of all races.

Suffrage as a Universal Right

THE UNITED NATIONS (UN), FOUNDED IN 1945, IS AN ORGANIZATION OF COUNTRIES that works for world peace and security and the betterment of humanity. Almost all of the world's independent countries belong to the UN. The UN has adopted many documents supporting women's rights. These documents are the bedrock of our modern system of human rights. Only 100 years ago, women's suffrage was considered a controversial issue. By the late 1900's, women had the right to vote in almost every country where men had the right. However, the story of women's suffrage still is not finished. Women in some countries of the world still face forms of discrimination that may make voting or holding public office difficult.

▶ The Universal Declaration of Human Rights sets forth basic civil, political, economic, social, and cultural rights and freedoms, including "universal and equal suffrage." The United Nations General Assembly adopted the declaration on Dec. 10, 1948. The document provides a common understanding of the rights and freedoms that every UN member country should promote and observe.

▼ Eleanor Roosevelt (1884-1962), the widow of U.S. President Franklin D. Roosevelt, views a copy of the Universal Declaration of Human Rights. She was part of the multinational committee that drafted the declaration.

1

Article 1

All human beings are born free and equal in dignity and rights. They are endowed with reason and conscience. . .

Article 21

1. Everyone has the right to take part in the government of his [or her] country, directly or through freely chosen representatives.

2. Everyone has the right to equal access to public service in his [or her] country.

3. The will of the people shall be the basis of the authority of government; this will shall be expressed in periodic and genuine elections which shall be by universal and equal suffrage and shall be held by secret vote or by equivalent free voting procedures.

from the Universal Declaration of Human Rights, 1948

3

Article 7

States Parties shall take all appropriate measures to eliminate discrimination against women in the political and public life of the country and, in particular, shall ensure to women, on equal terms with men, the right:

(a) To vote in all elections and public referenda and to be eligible for election to all publicly elected bodies;

(b) To participate in the formulation of government policy and the implementation thereof and to hold public office and perform all public functions at all levels of government;

(c) To participate in non-governmental organizations and associations concerned with the public and political life of the country.

from the Convention on the Elimination of All Forms of Discrimination Against Women, 1979

◀ The Convention on the Elimination of All Forms of Discrimination Against Women was adopted by the UN General Assembly on Dec. 18, 1979. Countries that accept the convention must commit to measures aimed at ending discrimination on the basis of sex, including discrimination in politics. Their laws must allow women to vote in all elections and stand for election to all publicly elected bodies.

4

▶ Kuwaiti women celebrate in May 2005 after the National Assembly (parliament) approved changes to Kuwait's electoral law, giving women the right to vote and to run in public elections. Although Kuwait's chief of state, the emir, issued a decree in 1999 that proposed giving women full political rights, Islamist members of parliament blocked changes to electoral law until 2005.

NOW YOU KNOW

- The United Nations has adopted many documents that support women's rights.
- Kuwaiti women gained suffrage in 2005.
- Nearly all nations today have formally given men and women equal voting rights.

Timeline

1791	Olympe de Gouges writes the Declaration of the Rights of Woman.
1792	Mary Wollstonecraft writes *A Vindication of the Rights of Woman.*
1837	Sarah Grimké writes "Letters on the Equality of the Sexes and the Condition of Women," serially published in the newspaper *The Spectator* in this year.
1848	The first women's rights convention in the United States meets at Seneca Falls, New York, and drafts the Declaration of Sentiments.
1851	Harriet Taylor Mill publishes "The Enfranchisement of Women;" Susan B. Anthony and Elizabeth Cady Stanton meet for the first time.
1867	Lydia Becker helps organize the Manchester National Society for Women's Suffrage, one of the first British suffrage organizations.
1869	John Stuart Mill publishes *The Subjection of Women.* American suffragists form the National Woman Suffrage Association (NWSA) and the American Woman Suffrage Association (AWSA). The Territory of Wyoming grants women suffrage.
1890	The NWSA and the AWSA merge to form the National American Woman Suffrage Association (NAWSA).
1893	New Zealand grants women suffrage in parliamentary elections. The state of Colorado gives women the vote.
1896	The state of Idaho gives women the vote.
1897	British suffrage societies join together to form the National Union of Women's Suffrage Societies (NUWSS).
1902	The Commonwealth of Australia gives women the right to vote in federal elections.
1903	British suffragists form the militant Women's Social and Political Union (WSPU).
1906	Finland becomes the first region in Europe to give women the right to vote.
1910	Women win the vote in the state of Washington.
1911	Women win suffrage in California.
1913	Norway grants women the right to vote and run in national elections.
1914	World War I begins and most women's suffrage groups suspend their suffragist activities.
1915	Denmark and Iceland give women the vote.
1916	Carrie Chapman Catt presents her Winning Plan at an NAWSA convention in Atlantic City, New Jersey
1917	Canada passes the Military Voters Act and the War-time Elections Act, extending suffrage to all military personnel and to female relatives of military men.
1918	The Representation of the People Act of 1918 extends suffrage to women over 30 in the United Kindom, including Ireland. Canada gives all women over 21 the right to vote in federal elections.
1919	Lady Astor, the first woman to serve in the British Parliament, is elected to the House of Commons.
1920	The 19th Amendment to the U.S. Constitution extends suffrage to women who are 21 and older.
1922	Ireland becomes a British dominion and Irish women win suffrage on the same terms as men.
1928	The Representation of the People Act of 1928 gives British women suffrage on the same terms as men.
1930	White women win suffrage in South Africa.
1937	Filipino women win suffrage in a special referendum in which only women may vote.
1948	The United Nations (UN) General Assembly adopts the Universal Declaration of Human Rights.
1950-1980	Dozens of new independent countries come into existence in Africa, and most of these give men and women equal voting rights.
1971	Switzerland grants women suffrage.
1979	The UN General Assembly adopts the Convention on the Elimination of All Forms of Discrimination Against Women.
1994	South Africa holds its first all-race election and nonwhite women are allowed to vote.
2005	Kuwait's National Assembly grants women suffrage and the right to run for public office.

Sources

4-5 Document 1 – Adams, John, and Abigail Adams. *Familiar Letters of John Adams and His Wife Abigail Adams, During the Revolution.* New York: Hurd and Houghton, 1876. *Google Books.* Web. 22 June 2010.
6-7 Document 1 – Talleyrand-Périgord, Charles Maurice de. Report to the National Constituent Assembly. 1791. Quoted in Kelly, Linda. *Women of the French Revolution.* London: Hamilton, 1989. Print. Document 2: Gouges, Olympe de. "Declaration of the Rights of Woman." 1791. In Levy, Darlene G., et al. *Women in Revolutionary Paris, 1789-1795.* University of Illinois Press, 1980. Print.
8-9 Document 2 – Wollstonecraft, Mary. *A Vindication of the Rights of Women.* 1792. London: T. F. Unwin, 1891. *Google Books.* Web. 22 June 2010. Document 4 – Burns, Robert. "The Rights of Woman." 1792. *Robert Burns Country.* Web. 24 June 2010.
10-11 Document 1 – "Address of the Female Political Union of Newcastle-upon-Tyne to Their Fellow Countrywomen." *Northern Star* [Leeds, Eng.] 9 Feb. 1839: 6. *Nineteenth-Century Serials Edition.* Web. 24 June 2010. Document 3 – Richardson, Reginald J. *The Rights of Women.* 1840. In *The Early Chartists.* Univ. of S. Carolina Pr., 1971. Print.
12-13 Document 1 – Grimké, Sarah M. Letters in *The Spectator.* 1837. Available at *Sunshine for Women.* Web. 24 June 2010. Document 4 – Stanton, Elizabeth Cady. *Eighty Years and More (1815-1897).* New York: European Pub. Co., 1897. *Google Books.* Web. 24 June 2010.
14-15 Document 1 – Declaration of Sentiments. 19 July 1848. In *Documents of American History: Volume I, to 1898.* Englewood Cliffs, NJ: Prentice Hall, 1988. Print. Document 2 – Stanton, Elizabeth Cady. Speech at the first Woman Suffrage Convention. 1869. In *History of Woman Suffrage.* Vol. 2. Rochester, NY: Susan B. Anthony, 1887. *Google Books.* Web. 24 June 2010.
16-17 Document 2 – *An Account of the Proceedings on the Trial of Susan B. Anthony . . .* Rochester, NY: Daily Democrat and Chronicle Book Print, 1874. *Google Books.* Web. 24 June 2010. Document 3 – Declaration of Rights for Women. 4 July 1876. In *History of Woman Suffrage.* Vol. 3. Rochester, NY: Susan B. Anthony, 1887. *Google Books.* Web. 24 June 2010.
18-19 Document 1 – Dilke, Charles W. Speech to Parliament. 4 May 1870. In *Hansard's Parliamentary Debates.* Vol. 201. T.C. Hansard, 1870. *Google Books.* Web. 29 June 2010. Document 3 – Mill, John Stuart. *The Subjection of Women.* Longmans, 1869. *Google Books.* Web 24 June 2010. Document 4 – Mill, Harriet Taylor. "The Enfranchisement of Women." *Westminster Review* July 1851: 149-61. *Google Books.* Web. 24 June 2010.
20-21 Document 1 – Queen Victoria. Letter to Theodore Martin. 1870. Quoted in Strachey, Lytton. *Queen Victoria.* New York: Harcourt, 1921. *Google Books.* Web. 24 June 2010. Document 3 – Disraeli, Benjamin. Speech. 27 Apr. 1866. Quoted in Blackburn, Helen. *Women's Suffrage.* London: Williams & Norgate, 1902. *Google Books.* Web. 24 June 2010.
22-23 Document 1 – Willard, Frances E. "The National Outlook in the Temperance Reform." *Our Day* Dec. 1892: 866-83. *Google Books.* Web. 24 June 2010. Document 2 – Gage, Matilda J. "Indian Citizenship." *National Citizenship and Ballot Box* May 1878: n. pag. Quoted in *Votes for Women.* Ed. Jean H. Baker. New York: Oxford, 2002. Print.
24-25 Document 1 – Sheppard, Kate. Letter to Sir John Hall. 1888. In Grimshaw, Patricia. *Women's Suffrage in New Zealand.* Auckland Univ. Pr., 1972. Print. Document 3 – Burn, David Will. M. "The Glorious 19th." *North Otago Times* 21 Sept. 1893: 3. *Papers Past.* Web. 24 June 2010.
26-27 Document 1 – Lawson, Louisa. Article in *Dawn* [journal edited by Lawson]. 1889. In *The First Voice of Australian Feminism.* Brookvale: Simon & Schuster, 1990. Print. Document 2 – Suffragist advertisement in the *Sydney Morning Herald.* 31 July 1901. In Oldfield, Audrey. *Woman Suffrage in Australia.* Cambridge University Press, 1992.
28-29 Document 1 – Gripenberg, Alexandra. "The Great Victory in Finland." *Englishwoman's Review* 16 July 1906: 155-57. In *Women, the Family, and Freedom.* Stanford Univ. Pr., 1983. Print. Document 3 – Sandal, Marta. Quoted in an article in the *Morning Albertan* [Calgary] 21 Feb. 1913: n. pag. *Great Norwegians.* Web. 24 June 2010.
30-31 Document 1 – Christabel Pankhurst and Annie Kenney. Questions asked at a Liberal Party meeting in Manchester. 13 Oct. 1905. Quoted in Pankhurst, Emmeline. *My Own Story* . London: Eveleigh Nash, 1914. Print. Document 3 – Fawcett, Millicent Garrett. Open letter to suffrage movement. Jan. 1906. In *The Women's Suffrage Movement: A Reference Guide, 1866-1928.* New York: Routledge, 2001. Print.
32-33 Document 1 – Mills, Theodora. "Rise Up Women!" In *Literature of the Women's Suffrage Campaign in England.* Peterborough, Ont.: Broadview, 2004. Print. Document 3 – Pankhurst, Emmeline. "Freedom or Death." 13 Nov. 1913. *Guardian.co.uk.* Web. 25 June 2010.
34-35 Document 1 – Anthony, Susan B. Letter to Elizabeth Cady Stanton. Oct. 1902. In *The History of Woman Suffrage.* Vol. 5. [New York]: NAWSA, 1922. *Google Books.* Web. 25 June 2010. Document 3 – Catt, Carrie Chapman. Address to the NAWSA. 1902. In *Man Cannot Speak for Her.* New York: Greenwood, 1989. Print.
36-37 Document 1 – Pankhurst, Sylvia. 1911. Quoted in *Votes for Women.* New York: Oxford, 2002. Print. Document 3 – Verse printed on banner of the International Woman Suffrage Alliance. 1911. In "Our Banner." *International Alliance of Women.* Web. 25 June 2010.
38-39 Document 1 – Pankhurst, Emmeline. Circular letter. 13 Aug. 1914. In *The Women's Suffrage Movement: A Reference Guide, 1866-1928.* New York: Routledge, 2001. Print. Document 3 – Pankhurst, Sylvia. *The Home Front.* London: Hutchinson & Co. 1932. Print.
40-41 Document 1 – McClung, Nellie. *The Women's Parliament.* 1914. Quoted in Baldwin, Douglas. *Ideologies.* Toronto: McGraw Hill, 1997. Print. Document 3 – Murray, E. M. Personal recollection to Catherine L. Cleverdon. 19 Apr. 1943. In Cleverdon, Catherine L. *The Woman Suffrage Movement in Canada.* University of Toronto Press, 1974. Print.
42-43 Document 1 – Asquith, Herbert. Speech to Parliament. 14 Aug. 1916. In *The Parliamentary Debates.* Vol. 85. London: H.M.S.O., 1916. Print. Document 3 – Sennett, Maud Arncliffe. 1918. Quoted in Law, Cheryl. *Suffrage and Power.* New York: I. B. Tauris, 1997. Print.
44-45 Document 1 – Motto of the *Irish Citizen.* Quoted in Yeates, Pádraig. *Lockout: Dublin 1913.* New York: Palgrave, 2001. Print. Document 3 – Proclamation of the Irish Republic. 1916. In *The Irish question. Hearings Before the Committee on Foreign Affairs . . .* Washington: GPO, 1919. *Google Books.* Web. 25 June 2010.
46-47 Document 1 – Park, Maud W. *Front Door Lobby.* Boston: Beacon, 1960. Print. Document 4 – Constitution of the United States. Amendment 19. Ratified on 18 Aug. 1920. *The Avalon Project.* Web. 25 June 2010.
48-49 Document 1 – Shishkina-Iavein, Poliksena. Speech to leaders of Russia's provisional government. 20 Mar. 1917. Quoted in Edmondson, Linda H. *Feminism in Russia, 1900-17.* Stanford Univ. Pr., 1984. Print. Document 2 – Alzona, Encarnación. "The Hernando Bill." 10 Sept. 1930. Quoted in *Women's Suffrage in Asia.* New York: Routledge, 2004. Print. Document 4 – Legarda, Trinidad F. "Philippine Women and the Vote" *Philippine Magazine* 28.4 (1931): 163+. Print.
50-51 Document 1 – Gandhi, Mohandas. Article in *Young India* [Bombay] 21 July 1921. In *Selections from Gandhi.* Ahmedabad: Navajivan, 1948. Print. Document 3 – Reddy, S. Muthulakshmi. 1931. In Premalatha, P. N. *Nationalism and Women's Movement in South India, 1917-1947.* New Delhi: Gyan Pub., 2003. Print
52-53 Document 1 – Brunschvicg, Cécile. "Les Femmes et le suffrage." *L'Humanité* [Paris] 19 May 1919: n. pag. Quoted in *Suffrage and Beyond.* New York University Press, 1994. Print. Document 2 – Sánchez, Atilia. Quoted in an article in *Agitación femenina* [Bogotá, Col.] 1944. Article quoted in *Suffrage and Beyond.* New York University Press, 1994. Print.
54-55 Document 1 – *Report of the Committee on the Extension of the Franchise to Women.* Zanzibar: Govt. Printer, 1959. Print. Document 3 – Ojiambo, Julia. Interview. 1978. In *Third World Women Speak Out.* New York: Praeger, 1979. Print.
56-57 Document 1 – *Report of the Select Committee on Enfranchisement of Women.* Cape Town: Cape Times Ltd., 1926. Quoted in *Women and Gender in Southern Africa to 1945.* Ed. Cherryl Walker. Cape Town: D. Philip, 1990. Print. Document 2 – Federation of South African Women. Women's Charter. 17 Apr. 1954. In Walker, Cherryl. *Women and Resistance in South Africa.* London: Onyx Press, 1982. Print. Document 3 – Constitution of the Republic of South Africa. 1996. *South African Government Information.* Web. 28 June 2010.
58-59 Document 1 – The Universal Declaration of Human Rights. 1948. *United Nations.* Web. 28 June 2010. Document 3 – Convention on the Elimination of All Forms of Discrimination Against Women. 1979. *United Nations.* Web. 28 June 2010.

Additional resources

Books

International Encyclopedia of Women's Suffrage, edited by June Hannam, Katherine Holden, and Mitzi Auchterlonie, ABC-CLIO, 2000

Right to Vote, by Deanne Durrett, Facts on File, 2005

Votes for Women, by Diane Atkinson, Cambridge University Press, 1989

Women's Suffrage, edited by Richard Haesly, Greenhaven, 2001

Women's Suffrage in America, by Elizabeth Frost-Knappman and Kathryn Cullen-Dupont, Facts on File, 2004

Websites

http://www.bbc.co.uk/history/british/abolition/abolition_women_article_01.shtml
This British Broadcasting Company (BBC) website discusses women's involvement in the abolition movement and the women's suffrage movement.

http://www.dhr.history.vt.edu/modules/eu/mod02_vote/index.html
This website created by historians and educators at Virginia Polytechnic Institute and State University contains commentary and online resources on women's suffrage in Europe.

http://www.rochester.edu/SBA/suffragehistory.html
A website by the Anthony Center for Women's Leadership at the University of Rochester. It contains information about suffrage history in the United States and short biographies of American suffragists.

http://teacher.scholastic.com/activities/suffrage/
This website created by the Scholastic publishing company explores the history of women's suffrage around the world.

Index

Index

Acknowledgments

Archives New Zealand: 24; Art Archive: 16, 34, 35 (Culver Pictures), 30, 33 (Museum of London), 38 (Museum of the City of New York/43.40.128), 42 (Eileen Tweedy); Bridgeman Art Library: 11; Castro, Alex R.: 49; Corbis: 9, 13, 20, 28, 32, 39, 44, 47, 50 (Bettmann), 29 (Underwood & Underwood/Bettman), 31, 53 (Hulton-Deutsch Collection), 37 (David J. & Janice Frent Collection), 45 (Sean Sexton Collection), 51 (Jitendra Prakash/Reuters), 57 (Jon Hrusa/epa); Getty: 19 (Hulton Archive), 23 (Topical Press Agency/Hulton Archive), 43 (Time & Life Pictures) 59 (Yasser Al-Zayyat/AFP); Library and Archives Canada: 40, 41; Library of Congress: 15; Mary Evans: 10, 18 (Grosvenor Prints), 21 (Illustrated London News Ltd), 36; Topfoto: 5, 7, 8, 12 (The Granger Collection), 25, 27. (FotWare Foto Station), 54 (AP), 55, 58 (Topham/UN).

Cover main image: Getty (AFP); inset image: Mary Evans